Praises for "Living Between"

"What could be more important than having the right tools to pass along the living hope and love of Jesus Christ to the next generation? This creative, thoughtful, biblical, and culturally tailored curriculum for Korean North American youth is just such a tool, meeting a very real need that no other resource does in such an accessible way. I have no doubt it will stimulate conversations and insights that move Korean North American youth to deeper levels of understanding, community, and faith."

-Dr. Mark Labberton, President of Fuller Theological Seminary

"The stories of Scripture and North American Korean teenagers find common ground in this remarkable and contextual curriculum. I can't imagine a better path to the hearts of our young people than through this perceptive and faithful gathering of lessons which speak eloquently of God's amazing grace."

-Dr. Gregg A. Mast, President of New Brunswick Theological Seminary

"Many thanks to G2G Center for producing this wonderful curriculum! I believe that *Living Between* will be a great tool and resource to raise up the next generation of faithful Korean North American Christians. It will help many Korean North American youth to develop deeper and stronger relationships with the triune God, the Korean North American church, and the global world that is in need of caring and faithful leaders."

-Rev. Mark Young Ho Ro, Education Pastor of Young Nak Presbyterian Church, LA

"The Korean North American community has long awaited a contextual curriculum that speaks truly to the Korean North American youth. This Bible study curriculum, 'Living Between,' addresses the specific needs of the Korean North American youth in ways that are cogent, relevant, and nurturing. This is an excellent resource for churches and parachurch organizations that work with Korean North American youth who are indeed "living between" the cultural boundaries!"

-Dr. Kirsten S. Oh, Assistant Professor of Practical Theology, Azusa Pacific University

"The new curriculum 'Living Between' uses many relevant examples from the Korean North American context to help youth deal with the challenges and questions that they encounter in the development of their identity as Korean North American Christians, as well as future leaders in the community. I highly recommend this curriculum for the churches."

-Hyepin Im, President of the Korean Churches for Community Development, LA.

"This resource offers a much needed series of lessons for adolescents in navigating the complexities of being a daughter or son of Korean immigrant parents. The strength of this curriculum is its linking of the Korean North American context to the Bible through the use of powerful stories of faith. Beyond this, it is a lived faith that the authors promote, so that youth will have the opportunity to reflect on how these stories are enacted as disciples of Christ today."

-Dr. Kathy L. Dawson, Associate Professor of Christian Education, Columbia Theological Seminary

"Hak Joon Lee and colleagues have created a new and historic resource uniquely dedicated to encouraging the faithful discipleship of Korean American young people. For years those who serve in Korean American contexts who have had to rely on synthesizing or re-writing curriculum to contextualize their ministry, now there is a current resource written by and for those serving in Korean American churches that helps resolve this need."

-Dr. Chap Clark, Professor of Youth, Family, and Culture, Fuller Theological Seminary

LIVING BETWEEN

A Christian Curriculum for Korean North American Youth

Edited by

Hak Joon Lee, Kevin Park, Kil Jae Park

G2G
Christian Education Center

Equipping generations of Asian American Christian leaders through education and empowerment.

The image of a tree on the cover page is based on a Korean ancient poem in 용비어천가 ("Yong-bi-uh-chun-ga"), which is the first work written in *hangul* (Korean) that was compiled during the time of King Sejong the Great.

"불휘 기픈 남간 바람에 아니 뮐세"
(뿌리가 깊은 나무는 나람에 흔들리지 않으니, 꽃이 좋고 열매가 많으니)
"*A deeply-rooted tree does not waver at wind, its flower blossoms, its fruit plentiful.*"

The tree symbolizes the life of our Korean North American youth who are deeply rooted in the Word of God and the Korean Church tradition, nurtured by the loving care of their parents and mentors, and thriving out of their bicultural experiences.

Published 2014 by
G2G Christian Education Center
2457 Santa Anita Ave, Altadena CA 91001
(646) 220-3258
g2gcec@gmail.com
www.g2gcenter.org

ISBN: 978-1-63173-517-2

Book designed by Sarah Pak (sarahypak0830@gmail.com)

G2G Christian Education Center
G2G Christian Education Center is a nonprofit Christian organization, founded in 2007 to address the spiritual, cultural, and social concerns in the Asian American Community.

To

Korean North American Parents
whose sacrifice and love for their children are truly inspirational and one of a kind,

Youth Pastors and Teachers
who untiringly journey together with our teenagers through their dark valleys and to their mountain tops, and

Korean North American Teenagers
whose potentials are truly unlimited in God.

Contents

Foreword

Frustration, uneasiness, worry, anxiety, desperation. These may be some of the words that best describe what Korean churches and their leaders in North America feel when they ponder upon their next generation. The book of Judges once noted a similar situation that happened to the Israelites. "After that whole generation had been gathered to their fathers, another generation grew up, who knew neither the LORD nor what he had done for Israel" (Judges 2:10). The writer of the book of Judges did not use the word, "NEXT," but used a rather thought provoking expression to describe the succeeding generation. The word used is, "ANOTHER."

"Next" implies continuity. "Another" does not. One generation knew the Lord. They knew what God had done for them. The generation that succeeded the previous generation did not.

This spells trouble. Hence the feelings of frustration, uneasiness, worry, anxiousness, desperateness and so on. So, what are we, as Korean churches in North America, to do about this trouble? Teach, pray, worship, evangelize, live, and be a model for the succeeding generation? Yes! But the concept that encompasses all of these things is *education*!

To aid the education of our succeeding generation to be a "next" generation, rather than "another" generation, G2G and KODIA have put together a long awaited curriculum titled Living Between.

As far as I know, this is the first of its kind in Korean churches in North America. God raised up a group of faithful servants to make this project possible. I would like to express my sincere gratitude to Professor Hak Joon Lee and other G2G staff members, the editors and writers of this curriculum, and the congregation of Milal Church in Toronto whose generosity and fervent prayer made all this possible.

May God use this small tool to make our NEXT generation know the Lord!

Rev. Sung Hwan No
Senior Pastor of Milal Church
Founder of KODIA

Acknowledgement

After the publication of *iDentity* in 2011, G2G Christian Center received many encouraging words and affirmations, with many agreeing to the desperate need for a contextual curriculum for Korean North American youths. Building upon their support and prayers, this curriculum, *Living Between* is written for the 10th grade Korean North American youths—the first of a three-part series curriculum that comprehensively covers a high school bible study for 10th through 12th graders.

Many people helped to make this curriculum possible. First and foremost our gratitude goes to KODIA and Rev. Sung Hwan No of Milal Church in Toronto, who provided a generous financial support for the entire curriculum project. In particular, Rev. No's and Milal Church's vision for the next generation is inspiring and empowering. G2G Center feels richly blessed to be partnering with them for the Kingdom.

It was my personal pleasure to work with 16 writers (Angela Ryo, Cecilia Yoon, Edward Yang, Grace Goodman, Hannah Lee, Irene Cho, Joseph Kim, Joshua Nam, Kevin Park, Kil Jae Park, Rebekah Lee, Sharon Kim, Sharon Hong—all 1.5 or second generation Korean North Americans; Ingrid Melendez, a Latina who is called to and currently serves at a Korean American Church; and Brian White, who married a Korean American woman, Sara, and has been serving a Korean immigrant church over the past 5 years). These writers represent diverse regions and denominations of North America, and all have extensive ministry experiences in Korean immigrant and/or EM churches. Their passion, imagination, and creativity are astounding—giving a new hope for the future of Korean North American Christian communities.

I also cannot express enough thanks for the hard work, passion, and commitment of the G2G staff, Rebekah Lee, Hannah Lee, and Joseph Kim. Their energy and love for the Korean North American churches and their young brothers and sisters are simply unsurpassable. I have been deeply encouraged by their commitment and services.

I also want to thank my friend Rev. E.J. Emerson for her edits, helpful comments and suggestions for the final draft that go beyond the ordinary responsibility of a copy editor.

My deepest gratitude goes to my friends and co-editors Kil Jae and Kevin whose wisdom and theological acumen were indispensable in bringing the curriculum into its current form. I am very glad that through the *iDentity* project and the current project, our friendship and camaraderie have deepened together with the passion for Asian North American churches.

My hope is that every Korean North American youth will truly enjoy this curriculum and build enduring friendships with other members of the youth group, as Daniel and his friends did. They are our future and really the reason why we produce this curriculum.

Hak Joon Lee
President
G2G Christian Education Center

Introduction

"A goose family" in Korean idiom does not refer to a tribe of migrating birds frequently observed in the North East Asia. It metaphorically describes a married couple virtually living in separation, sometimes for a decade, between Korea and the U.S or Canada simply to offer a better education to their children. A goose father is usually working in South Korea to financially support the family overseas, while a goose mother takes care of the children who attend schools in the U.S. or Canada. The idiom came from the fact that a father must travel a long distance, often only once a year, to see his family. As the New York Times reported and President Obama also mentioned, this zeal for education is shockingly weird in the eyes of North Americans. They are surprised to find that behind this unusual family practice is the unique Asian cultural tradition where the parents sacrifice to provide the best education for their children. If they can afford it, many Koreans want to send their children to the U.S. and Canada for their studies as they believe a good education is a stepping-stone for the successful professional and economic future of their children, especially in this time of a competitive global economy.

In response to this cultural passion, therefore, many private educational institutes (*hakwon*) are mushrooming in Koreantowns where many new immigrants bring their children for an educational purpose. Even non-Christian parents do not mind sending their children to the church for the study of *hangul* and other educational programs and events. When a local church wants to build a new sanctuary, education is a major pitch point of its leaders; they need a new spacious facility to provide a better education for Korean children. And it works because many immigrants came to educate their children. Immigrant parents laugh or weep according to the success or failure of their children. In short, for Korean immigrants, education is *the* roadmap to the American Dream.

However, behind this collective passion for education are many broken dreams, parent-child conflicts, and cultural confusions. Such pain and suffering do not discriminate between Christians or non-Christians. The gap between Korean and North American cultures, generational discrepancies, and language barriers present enormous challenges to parents and children, teachers and pastors. Our children, youths in particular, are stuck in the middle between Korea and North America, home and school, church and secular culture, usually without proper role models, wise mentors, and reliable spiritual and moral guidance. The second-generation youths feel disconnected and isolated despite the sharing of the physical space with their parents at home and in church. Some of our children may be academically successful, but are still psychologically, emotionally, and spiritually struggling. Our children desperately need a spiritual vision and moral wisdom that will enable them to navigate between these conflicting forces. Many first generation parents and pastors feel frustrated and even powerless because of cultural and generational limitations and lack of educational resources.

This curriculum responds to these dire needs of our Korean North American community. Contextually grounded, it is specially designed to address the issues facing and being experienced by Korean North American youths: salvation, prayer, body image, addiction, relationship with parents, friends, character, K-Pop, and so on. This curriculum assists youths to freely encounter, engage, and explore the issues of their teen life on their own terms.

Our curricular spirit and philosophy is similar to that of the Talmud. Diaspora Jews in the last two millennia, despite constant marginalization and persecution, have been able to keep their identity and sustain their people through religious education in synagogues. The Torah and Talmud instilled inner strength and wisdom to cope with the challenges of their lives. It should be noticed that the Talmud touches not only spiritual concerns, but also every tough, complex issue of life from the perspective of faith. It deals with all aspects of human life on the basis of belief that God is the Lord and Creator of the Universe, and His reign takes place in every inch of the world.

The "4Cs" constitute the organizing principles of the curriculum: Christ, culture, competence (or gifts), and community, which we believe are the core factors that shape the life of Korean North American youths. The curriculum is roughly divided into these four areas and 16 writers have contributed differently to each area, according to their gifts, passion, and experiences.

In addressing these issues we have made every effort to be socially attentive and culturally inclusive, given our context. Some chapters may resonate closely with your group, and others may not. We ask for patience in your journey with your students, seeking deeper knowledge of God and growth in Christ through this curriculum.

It is our prayer that this curriculum be used to share wonderful spiritual blessings and testimonies of the first generation Korean North Americans with their beloved children, so that their lives are fulfilled and thriving in this land for the glory of God's kingdom and pride of their parents and pastors.

LESSON 1

"Three Words: Jesus Loves You"

Story[1]

Richard had just immigrated to America during the summer, and began his 9th grade year. Walking home from school one day, he saw a drunken man yelling outside the doors of a church. The man spotted Richard and started running toward him! Richard was frozen in fear when all of a sudden, the man shouted, "Punch me!!"

What?

"Punch me, and I'll give you money!!" Richard was confused and struggled to respond to him appropriately in English. Glancing at the church in the background, Richard spoke the only words that were clear at that moment, "Jesus loves you." The man violently screamed, "No! Jesus doesn't love me!" Richard wanted to agree with the man and just get out of the situation, but he found himself repeating to the man, "Jesus loves you." The man started punching the walls of the church, weeping and yelling, "How can You do this? No one loves me! No one will ever love me again! You can't love me."

After a moment, the man slumped down, looked at Richard and told him everything. The man had committed a serious sin that led to a divorce. His wife and kids left him, and everything in his life fell apart. In his pain and bitterness, he got drunk and wandered into the streets until he came to this church. In desperation, the man had prayed, "God, if You still love me, then send someone to tell me so." When he saw Richard he was merely hoping to get beat up so to ease the pain in his heart. He wasn't expecting God to respond with love, especially after all he had done.

Richard's experience that day transformed the way he understood God's love. It probably transformed the other man's life, too.

Questions

1. What do you find to be surprising about this story?

2. Do you think that God answered the man's prayer? If so, why do you think God answered him?

Summary

We normally think that good and successful people deserve love, and bad people deserve punishment. This story is surprising because God loved someone who considered himself to be a failure, totally unworthy of His love.

1 Based on a true story of one of the authors.

Text

Romans 5:6-8

*[6] You see, at just the right time, when we were still powerless, Christ
died for the ungodly. [7] Very rarely will anyone die for a righteous person,
though for a good person someone might possibly dare to die. [8] But God
demonstrates his own love for us in this: While we were still sinners,
Christ died for us.*

Questions

1. In v. 6, it says Christ died for the ungodly. What is your understanding of "ungodly"? Can you describe some ungodly people? Why is it surprising that Christ died for the ungodly?

2. The Bible says, "While we were still sinners, Christ died for us." Why is this timing of His death important in understanding God's love?

Application

1. Was there a time you experienced God's love when you felt that you did not deserve it?

2. Give examples of ways you can apply God's unconditional love in your own life in relationship to other people (e.g., caring for someone mean or annoying, forgiving someone who has disappointed or hurt you in the past, etc.).

LESSON 2

"Gwan Soon Yoo (1902-1920): A Girl Who Moved the Nation"

Story

Last summer, Grace visited her grandmother in Korea. During her stay there, she had a chance to visit the Korean Independence Museum in city of Cheonan. Among many displays, what caught her attention the most was the story of Gwan Soon Yoo, a teenage martyr of the March 1st Independence movement in 1919. Though familiar with the Civil Rights Movement and Dr. Martin Luther King, Jr., Grace had never heard about the 1919 Movement, which involved Korean Christians. Like the Civil Rights Movement, they used a nonviolent method to resist the injustices of the Japanese occupation of Korea. Here is a brief story of the young hero that Grace learned about:

Gwan Soon Yoo grew up in a Christian family. Her father and mother were very faithful Christians and her uncle was a minister (JDSN) of her home church. It is said that her father always prayed for his five children, that they would serve people and the nation through their studies and work. During her study at Ewha Women's High School, a Methodist mission school in Seoul, Gwan Soon actively participated in the Movement with her classmates. When her school was forcibly closed by the Japanese colonial authority, she returned home in the Cheonan area and assisted her parents and church members organize a demonstration. They rallied in Aunae marketplace, her hometown, and it was one of the largest demonstrations of the Movement. However, Japanese military police opened fire on the crowd, killing nineteen people, including Gwan Soon's father and mother, and wounding many. Gwan Soon was also arrested and sentenced to three years of imprisonment, but prematurely died in the prison as a result of severe torture. She was only seventeen years old. Her courageous actions, despite her youth, were motivated by deep faith in God. Her parents, church, and Christian school had instilled in her the love of God and love for her people. Gwan Soon's faith and courage has inspired all Koreans in the following generations, both Christians and non-Christians.

Rosa Parks—A Woman Who Moved the South

Rosa Parks (1913-2005) was an African American woman who sparked the Montgomery Bus Boycott, the early major event in the Civil Rights Movement in the U.S., which introduced Rev. Martin Luther King, Jr. as a national and international moral leader.

On December 1, 1955, Rosa Parks, then a 42-year-old who worked as a seamstress, boarded a Montgomery City bus to return home from work. The segregation law did not allow blacks and whites to sit together. The front ten seats were always reserved for whites. When all of those seats were filled, then blacks were required to yield their seats to whites. On the December date, Rosa

Questions

1. (A) What is the most inspiring part of Gwan Soon's story? (B) What similarity do you see between Gwan Soon and Rosa Parks, a woman who sparked the Civil Rights Movement in the U.S.? (C) What was the source of their courage?

Parks was sitting just behind the white section, and when a white man entered the bus, the bus driver ordered her and three other blacks to give up their seats for the white man. Rosa Parks refused to give up her seat. She was quickly arrested and convicted of violating the segregation law, which she appealed, challenging the legality of the law.

Although her action of civil disobedience in the bus was spontaneous, she had a strong sense of justice. She was then secretary of the local NAACP (the National Association for the Advancement of Colored People), the nation's oldest civil rights organization, and had recently received training for racial equality and worker's rights at the Highlander Folk School in Tennessee. As a consequence of her act, she was fired from her job as a seamstress in a local department store. However, she was later recognized nationally and internationally for her courageous work as a civil rights activist, including the receipt of the Presidential Medal of Freedom and the Congregational Gold Medal.

2. Gwan Soon died because of her protest against the Japanese colonial rule. What do you think about Christians participating in a peaceful protest against injustice?

Summary

Christian faith is personal, but not private. Christians are called to be salt and light in the world. As we serve God, the Maker of heaven and earth, the Lord who rules the universe with love and justice, we should practice justice and actively stand against injustice using peaceful means. The early Korean Christians understood this truth and lived it out faithfully. As a result, they were highly respected by their fellow citizens, and many people in fact converted to the Christian faith.

Text

Romans 12: 17-21

[17] *Do not repay anyone evil for evil. Be careful to do what is right in the eyes*
of everyone. [18] *If it is possible, as far as it depends on you, live at peace*
with everyone. [19] *Do not take revenge, my dear friends, but leave room for*
God's wrath, for it is written: "It is mine to avenge; I will repay," says the
Lord. [20] *On the contrary:*
"If your enemy is hungry, feed him;
if he is thirsty, give him something to drink.
In doing this, you will heap burning coals on his head."
[21] *Do not be overcome by evil, but overcome evil with good.*

Questions

1. What does the text teach about how Christians should respond in the face of evil (see vv. 17, 19, 21)? How did Gwan Soon exemplify/live out these principles in her actions during the March 1st Movement?

2. What does it mean to "overcome evil with good?" How is it different from "revenge" or repaying "evil with evil"? Why is it important to resist evil rather than tolerate it?

Food for Thought

A study shows that non-violent campaigns are more effective than violent resistance, even when used against similar opponents. According to Maria Stephan and Erica Chenoweth, social movements between 1900 and 2006 that relied on non-violent campaigns succeeded 53% of the time, while violent means succeeded only 26% of the time. One well-known example of the success is the Civil Rights Movement in the U.S.[2]

Application

Take as an example one form of injustice (e.g., poverty, racism, sexism, immigration, ecological degradation) prevailing in our society. Discuss how you could overcome it with good.

2 Source: Maria J. Stephan and Erica Chenoweth. "Why Civil Resistance Works: The Strategic Logic of Nonviolent Conflict." *International Security* 33, no. 1 (Summer 2008): 7-44.

LESSON 3

"Who Would Love Me?"

Story

Kevin sat alone at lunch. He didn't feel like talking to anyone today. All of his friends were busy thinking of ways to ask girls to the homecoming dance, and he was pretty sure he wasn't going to go. "*What girl would like me?*" he thought. He flashed back to P.E. class—his least favorite subject. He was skinnier and shorter than the non-Asian boys in his grade. Some of them already had muscles in their arms and abs like the pro players on television. And even though his mom told him that she thought he was handsome, Kevin knew he didn't look anything like the male actors in those dramas she was always watching. Kevin sighed and finished eating his lunch. He was not going to the dance.

Questions

1. Why do you think Kevin cares if he looks as strong as other guys in his class or as "handsome" as the guys in Korean dramas?

2. Kevin's image of beauty is being shaped by several different influences. What are those influences? What are some other people/things that influence your own image of beauty?

[Optional Activity]

Give each student a piece of paper and a pen or pencil. Ask them to write down as many different things they can think of that influence the way they think about beauty (or being handsome). For example, in the story about Kevin, we can see how our classmates and television shows like Korean dramas can influence what we think being "handsome" looks like.
When they are done, ask them to circle the influences that are most important to them. Next, have them flip over their piece of paper. On the back have the students write, "A beautiful/handsome person is..." and then write as many different descriptive words they can think of to describe a beautiful person. For example, a student might write, "A handsome person is *strong, tall, kind... etc.*" When they are done, ask them to circle the words they think apply to themselves.

[Activity Questions]

1. Which influences did you circle on your list? Why are these the most important to you?

2. Share your descriptions of beauty with the group. Do you mostly agree with what others have written, or disagree? Why?

Summary

Just like Kevin from the story, we all have a desire to be loved and accepted. That is why we care about society's definition of beauty/handsomeness, which society equates to worth. We want others to consider us worthy in order to be loved and accepted by them. The Bible recognizes this need that we all have. It points us, however, to a deeper source of acceptance than external standards of worth: God's steadfast love for us.

Text

Judges 6:11-16

11 The angel of the Lord came and sat down under the oak in Ophrah
that belonged to Joash the Abiezrite, where his son Gideon was threshing
wheat in a winepress to keep it from the Midianites. 12 When the angel of
the Lord appeared to Gideon, he said, "The Lord is with you, mighty war-
rior."
13 "Pardon me, my lord," Gideon replied, "but if the Lord is with us, why has
all this happened to us? Where are all his wonders that our ancestors told
us about when they said, 'Did not the Lord bring us up out of Egypt?' But
now the Lord has abandoned us and given us into the hand of Midian."
14 The Lord turned to him and said, "Go in the strength you have and save
Israel out of Midian's hand. Am I not sending you?"
15 "Pardon me, my lord," Gideon replied, "but how can I save Israel? My
clan is the weakest in Manasseh, and I am the least in my family."
16 The Lord answered, "I will be with you, and you will strike down all the
Midianites, leaving none alive."

Romans 8:31-39

31 What, then, shall we say in response to these things? If God is for us,
who can be against us? 32 He who did not spare his own Son, but gave him
up for us all—how will he not also, along with him, graciously give us all
things? 33 Who will bring any charge against those whom God has chosen?
It is God who justifies. 34 Who then is the one who condemns? No one.
Christ Jesus who died—more than that, who was raised to life—is at the
right hand of God and is also interceding for us. 35 Who shall separate us

from the love of Christ? Shall trouble or hardship or persecution or famine
or nakedness or danger or sword? 36 *As it is written:*
"For your sake we face death all day long;
we are considered as sheep to be slaughtered."
37 *No, in all these things we are more than conquerors through him who*
loved us. 38 *For I am convinced that neither death nor life, neither angels*
nor demons, neither the present nor the future, nor any powers, 39 *neither*
height nor depth, nor anything else in all creation, will be able to separate
us from the love of God that is in Christ Jesus our Lord.

Questions

1. In Judges 6:12, the angel calls Gideon, "mighty warrior." How is the angel's view of Gideon radically different from Gideon's view of himself?

2. Why do you think Gideon considered himself unworthy and inadequate for the task the angel called him to do?

3. According to the Romans passage, what is the source of our worth and strength?

Food for Thought

How will the experience of God's love help us to gain self-esteem?

- Receiving God's love and acceptance helps you value yourself more
- When you value and respect yourself more, you gain better self-confidence
- When you have more self-confidence, you will gain more respect from others
- While not everyone in this world will change their mind about you, when you walk tall in the love of God, people will find it attractive and will want to know the source of your confidence.

Application

1. How do you think it could help Kevin to know that he is loved and accepted by God?

2. What are three ways you can help encourage others who are struggling like Kevin?

4

LESSON

"Mountain Dew Worship"

Story

James woke up abruptly. He was so tired, but his mom was yelling for him to get dressed. It was Sunday, but the last place James wanted to be was church. He just wanted to sleep.

James had been going to church as long as he could remember. His father was a deacon; his mother was a teacher in the children's ministry; he was a member of the praise team. But the truth was, he just kind of felt obligated to go. He knew his parents would be disappointed if he didn't. Their friends would ask where he was. He knew the praise team needed him. He knew some of his friends would miss seeing him there. He also felt that God was important, but it was hard to say exactly why. And so he went every Friday and every Sunday.

"*But just once*," James thought to himself as he pulled on a shirt, "*it would be nice to sleep in*."

Questions

1. Name three reasons for why you think people come to church. What about you? Why do you come to church?

2. Have you ever felt like James, not really wanting to come to church? What are some reasons someone might not want to come to church?

Summary

A lot of times, instead of being a place where you can find comfort and be refreshed, church can feel like just one more thing that you have to do, one more obligation. But this isn't how the Bible describes Christian community. God doesn't want worship to be just one more obligation, one more burden on your already busy schedule. It is actually one of the main ways that God desires to bless and refresh you.

Text

Psalm 133

A song of ascents. Of David.

1 How good and pleasant it is when God's people live together in unity!

A "song of ascents," is a psalm written to be sung as the congregation of Israel was climbing up to the temple, which was at the top of a large hill in Jerusalem.

2 It is like precious oil poured on the head, running
down on the beard, running down on Aaron's beard,
down on the collar of his robe. 3 It is as if the dew
of Hermon were falling on Mount Zion. For there the
LORD bestows his blessing, even life forevermore.

Questions

1. Describe the differences between James' experience and King David's experience of worship.

2. David compares the experience of worship to Aaron being anointed with oil (v. 2). This oil is what consecrated and set Aaron apart as a priest (Exodus 30:30). Similarly, as Christians, we have been set apart by our adoption in Christ to serve God (1 Peter 2:9). How does worship help remind us of this?

Application

1. David uses the metaphors of an oily beard and mountain dew. What would you compare your own experience of your youth group/church community to? Why?

2. David loved the experience of worshipping in community because it gave him a sense of unity in serving God together with others. What is something that your church does that cultivates a sense of unity?

LESSON 5
"How Do I Know I'm Saved?"

Story

Even as a little kid in Korea, Yoonsoo always went to church with his family on Sundays. His mother was a very faithful Christian. His father was not religious at all, but went to church because he thought it was a good thing to do for the family. Yoonsoo was about ten when his family moved to Canada. They soon found a Korean church and began to attend regularly. This church, however, was quite different from Yoonsoo's old church in Korea. It seemed much more "into God;" worship services were livelier, longer, and the pastor preached louder with more conviction. It took Yoonsoo some time to get used to this different way of "doing" church.

During one Friday night service, Yoonsoo's father experienced God in a powerful way – he broke down crying and accepted Jesus as his Lord and Savior. That night, Yoonsoo's father took all his bottles of wine and liquor and poured them down the drain. He also tried to quit smoking, but that was much harder, and it took Yoonsoo's father almost a year to quit completely. There was a dramatic change in Yoonsoo's father's life. Yoonsoo could see that his father's conversion was genuine. He was going to church, not because he believed it was a "good thing to do for the family," but because he truly believed in God. Yoonsoo's conversion was not as dramatic as his father's was. Yoonsoo believed in God and believed that Jesus was God's only Son who died for him, but he wondered if he needed to have a conversion experience like his father's in order to become a "real" Christian.

Questions

1. When you think of your own faith experience, whom do you relate to more, Yoonsoo or his father?

2. Do you think there is only one right way of becoming a Christian? If you are already a self-confessing Christian, was your experience similar to Yoonsoo or his father?

Summary

The story illustrates two different ways of becoming and being a Christian. Some people come to believe in a gradual way like Yoonsoo who grew up in the church. Others come to faith in a more sudden and dramatic way like Yoonsoo's father. Some people may even go through aspects of both experiences. There is no one right experience of salvation. Although Yoonsoo believed in Jesus as his Lord, he began to question his faith when he saw his father's sudden and dramatic conversion. This story functions to facilitate a discussion about how we can be sure of our salvation.

Text

Romans 10:9-10 (NRSV)

[9]...if you confess with your lips that Jesus is Lord and believe in your heart
that God raised him from the dead, you will be saved. [10] For one believes
with the heart and so is justified, and one confesses with the mouth and
so is saved.

Questions

1. According to Romans 10:9, how are we saved? What do we have to confess and believe in order to be saved?

2. Verse 10 emphasizes the importance of believing in one's heart and confessing with one's mouth. Why do you think both are important?

3. Can you think of another well-known Bible verse that speaks about the assurance of salvation?

Application

1. How did you become a Christian? That is, how did you come to believe in Jesus as your Lord?

2. Make a covenant with each other to memorize Romans 10:9-10 during the next week, and encourage each other to meditate on the promise in the text and to claim it as your own.

6

LESSON

"To Mix or Not to Mix"

Story

James and David are both active members of their church youth group, and they both love music. But they have strong disagreements on what kind of music Christians should listen to. James enjoys listening to "secular" music that has a good beat. He also likes to point out that Christians have freedom in Christ to enjoy popular culture. David, on the other hand, has problems with Christians listening to any music that does not glorify God. He argues that "secular" music stirs unhealthy emotions for its listeners.

Activity

The Debate – "Should Christians listen to 'secular' music?"

Divide the students *randomly* into two groups (i.e., students might not be in the group that represents their own position on this issue).

Assign each group to debate the question of whether or not Christians should listen to "secular" music; one group taking James' position and the other group taking David's. After briefly discussing (about 5 minutes) among group members, each group should present supporting statements for their position.

Questions

1. Whom do you agree with more: James or David? Why? Why not the other?

2. If you agreed more with James, would you say that there is certain "secular" music that Christians should not listen to? If you agreed with David, do you think it is possible for music that makes no direct reference to God/Christ to still be honoring to God?

Summary

We cannot fully agree with James or David. Neither one is completely correct or completely wrong. There are times when we need to be like David by rejecting parts of our culture (whether it's particular music, movies, books, etc.) that are sinful. There are also times when we need to be like James by seeing value in parts of our culture that may agree with God's character and how God wants us to live. To do this, we need discernment to reject the sinful things within our culture and to recognize ways in which our culture can be helpful to us. It was with this in mind that Paul wrote to the church at Philippi, "*Finally, brothers and sisters, whatever is true, whatever is noble, whatever is right, whatever is pure, whatever is lovely, whatever is admirable—if anything is excellent or praiseworthy—think about such things*" (Philippians 4:8).

Text

Acts 17:16-17, 22-31

*[16] While Paul was waiting for them in Athens, he was greatly distressed to
see that the city was full of idols. [17] So he reasoned in the synagogue with
both Jews and God-fearing Greeks, as well as in the marketplace day by
day with those who happened to be there.*

*[22] Paul then stood up in the meeting of the Areopagus and said: "People of
Athens! I see that in every way you are very religious. [23] For as I walked
around and looked carefully at your objects of worship, I even found an
altar with this inscription: TO AN UNKNOWN GOD. So you are ignorant of the
very thing you worship—and this is what I am going to proclaim to you. [24]
"The God who made the world and everything in it is the Lord of heaven
and earth and does not live in temples built by human hands. [25] And he is
not served by human hands, as if he needed anything. Rather, he himself
gives everyone life and breath and everything else. [26] From one man he
made all the nations, that they should inhabit the whole earth; and he
marked out their appointed times in history and the boundaries of their
lands. [27] God did this so that they would seek him and perhaps reach out
for him and find him, though he is not far from any one of us. [28] 'For in him
we live and move and have our being.' As some of your own poets have
said, 'We are his offspring.' [29] "Therefore since we are God's offspring, we
should not think that the divine being is like gold or silver or stone—an
image made by human design and skill. [30] In the past God overlooked such
ignorance, but now he commands all people everywhere to repent. [31] For
he has set a day when he will judge the world with justice by the man he
has appointed. He has given proof of this to everyone by raising him from
the dead."*

Commentary

In this passage, we begin with Paul being troubled by the idolatry of the Athenians (v. 16). Instead of giving up on the people with their sinful practices, Paul saw an important task in teaching the truth of the gospel (v. 17). He is later invited to speak at Areopagus ("Ares Rock," also known as "Mars Hill"), which was a hilltop-gathering place for discussing new ideas.

While Paul made numerous citations from the Old Testament when preaching the gospel in other cities, he made no such citation when preaching in Athens. Rather, he mentioned products of Athenian culture to meet the people within their own cultural mindset and to show how God is active in leading people to Christ.

Questions

1. What was Paul's attitude toward Athenian culture? (Pick from list) Give reasons for your choice.
1) *rejecting completely* 2) *accepting/embracing* 3) *condoning* 4) *selectively engaging* 5) *ignoring*

2. Read vv. 23 & 28. What elements of Athenian culture did Paul use in his preaching at Areopagus? How did this method help Paul connect the Athenians to the gospel?

3. What can we learn from Paul's method?

Application

Were your personal views on "secular" music changed or reinforced through the debate activity and the bible study? In what ways? Do you recognize a need for greater discernment in your attitude toward popular culture?

7

LESSON

"Tough Love"

Story

Sean's Story

I know Joon's a good guy. He's been through a lot, but he can never seem to hold on to his friends. The thing though with him is that he doesn't know how to own up when he does something wrong, and he always plays the sympathy card. On our friend Steve's birthday, our group planned a surprise party. Joon offered to take care of it, but he messed up big time. It would have been okay if Joon apologized, but he went off about how it wasn't his fault and started talking about his past again. I don't like confrontation, but the other guys were going to give up on Joon, so I knew someone had to talk to him. He actually got pretty upset with me, and I wished I had kept my mouth shut. A week later, Joon called and thanked me. He said that no one had ever cared enough to be straight with him like that. He apologized to the guys, and things have started getting a lot better.

Questions

1. If you were Sean, what would you have done? Would you have confronted Joon? What aspects would have been challenging for you personally? Why?

2. Share about a time when you were on the receiving end of a hard truth. If you have never experienced this, share about a time when you wish you had been.

Summary

Being a good friend involves giving and accepting encouragement as well as loving correction. Friends build each other up in love and truth even when it can be difficult.

Text

Proverbs 27:5-6, 17

5 *Better is open rebuke than hidden love.*
6 *Wounds from a friend can be trusted, but an enemy multiplies kisses.*

17 *As iron sharpens iron, so one person sharpens another.*

Questions

1. What does Solomon mean by "hidden love?" How are verses 5 and 6 related?

2. What do you think "sharpening one another," means? What can that look like practically in your everyday relationships?

Application

When iron sharpens iron, there is inevitable friction. In the same way, correction can be easily misunderstood as criticism. Here are five practical tips on how to tell the truth in love:

Loving Confrontation: 5 Practical Tips

1. Timing is Everything.
Don't wait too long—"*Don't let the sun go down on your anger*" (Eph 4:26). Address conflict before it festers. Our culture influences the way we deal with conflict. Our Asian background makes us less likely to confront people. Sometimes, letting a situation blow over is both gracious and wise, but, at times, this causes negative feelings to build up in our hearts, making us prone to "blow up" in anger later.

2. Truly Care.
Let your friend know it is because you care that you are having this talk.

3. Use Indoor Voices.
It is never wise to approach this kind of conversation while angry. Make sure you're at peace before you begin, and take care not to raise your voice, even if things don't go the way you planned.

4. Check Yourself.
What is your desired outcome in this confrontation? Be honest. Is it more important for you to get your point across or for you to bring mutual growth in your relationship? Take some time to pray and examine your heart. The motivation for godly rebuke is always to promote mutual growth. This being said, your job in issuing rebuke is never to change your friend—that's God's job. Your job is to speak truth and love your friend through the process of change, however long that might take.

5. Listen. Then, Affirm.
How you felt in the situation or conflict was valid, but so was how your friend felt. Do your best to understand where the other person is coming from. Make it a rule not to interrupt while your friend speaks. Then validate the other person's feelings and experience of the situation. "*It must have been frustrating for you when...*" or "*I could see how that could have made you feel ______.*"

LESSON 8
"I Never Noticed"

Story

Sammy had been reluctant to invite his Caucasian friend Trevor to his Korean Canadian Church, but their weekend camping plan included going to church on Sunday, and Trevor was enthusiastic about visiting.

They went through the usual Sunday youth service, and then after service, headed over to the fellowship hall for lunch. As pungent smell of curry and kim-chee filled the room, Sammy began to worry that Trevor might be in for a culture shock.

"Oh my goodness. Is that curry?" asked Trevor. Just as Sammy was about to blush, Trevor yelled, "I LOVE CURRY! Is this a special day for something?"

Sammy answered, "No, this is just our usual Sunday lunch."

"You mean, you guys get lunch like this *every* week? Man, I wish our church would feed us real food. We usually split right after service, and have to hunt for food and fellowship. Dude, we should invite Greg next time. I'm sure he wouldn't mind listening to Jesus over a hot lunch!"

Questions

1. Is Trevor's reaction surprising to you? Why or why not?

2. Based on the story, what was the unique aspect of the Korean church that Trevor really appreciated?

Summary

Sammy did not recognize the great value of sharing a meal with his church every week. It's not that Sammy was ungrateful, but he had taken it for granted because it was a normal, customary thing in Korean North American churches. He had not realized how naturally his church expressed hospitality, and how much value it had in impacting and blessing members of the church and guests. This unique aspect of the Korean church made him appreciate his culture more, and he began to wonder if there were other gifts that he and his church had to offer.

Text

1 Peter 4:8-10

[8] Above all, love each other deeply, because love covers over a multitude of sins. [9] Offer hospitality to one another without grumbling. [10] Each of you should use whatever gift you have received to serve others, as faithful stewards of God's grace in its various forms.

Food for Thought

Statistical Information from the Korean Center for Community Development:[3]

- There are 4,000 Korean American Churches nationally

- In 2000, the 4 ethnic communities with income below the national median level were: African American, Latino, Native Indian, and *Korean.*

And yet...

- Top 5 Korean American Mega-Churches (5,000-8,000 members each) give an annual offering $15 million—this is 10 times the offering size of other ethnic churches of the same size (i.e., other mega churches give about $1.5 million on average).

- The largest portion of their offerings goes towards world missions, mainly in Africa, Latin America, and China.

- Churches in Korea send out more missionaries than any other country in the world, after the U.S.

- A survey of 16 Korean American churches show that they total over 45 different types of social and community services (e.g., child care, healthcare clinics and fairs, after school programs, scholarships, job training, domestic violence support and shelter, programs for the homeless, etc.)

Korean North American Churches are wells of blessings, ready to pour out to our community! Get more involved in acts of generosity, and make a difference *with* your church, *for* the world.

Questions

1. Peter exhorts Christians to offer hospitality (v. 9). What is hospitality, and why do you think it is something that the people of God should aspire to do?

2. What does it mean to steward? According to verse 10, what are we stewarding?

Application

Now that we understand the true value of hospitality, I don't know about you, but I'm proud to say that Korean North American Churches *know* how to do hospitality! Hospitality is a gift. When 1 Peter 4:10 says that we have received "gifts," it's not talking about skills and talents. A gift is an unmerited blessing that we received from others. Apostle Peter is saying that because we are blessed, we now have the ability to bless others in that same way. When we do exactly that, we are being the stewards God wants us to be.

Let's take a new look at your church with this knowledge. List two "gifts" your youth group (or your church) has received, and tell us how they can be used to serve others.

3 Stephanie C. Boddie and Hyepin Im. "Korean American Churches as Partners in Community Development: The Untold Story." http://kccd.org/sites/default/files/kccd_ka_churches_white_house_paper_092008_edit.pdf

9

LESSON

"Other Side of Sin"

Story

A couple of school bullies verbally and physically attacked a scrawny Asian kid who was obviously a JFK ("Just From Korea"). Jin was standing right there by the lockers and saw the whole thing. You could just tell that the Asian kid was a JFK. It was clear by the way he dressed, his haircut, his demeanor, even how he yelled, "Aye Ya!" when the bullies pushed him. The JFK was knocked to the floor with his books and notes sprawled all around him.

Jin really wanted to go and help the JFK... but he felt embarrassed and vulnerable. Jin was a pretty scrawny Korean kid himself. Who was he to help? He was no hero. Jin didn't want to draw attention to himself. Why should he help him when all the other kids just passed right by? Jin didn't want to stand out. Besides, if Jin helped him, the other kids might think that he was a JFK as well. Jin was born in the United States and considered himself way more American than Korean. He definitely WASN'T a JFK. Although a part of him really felt sorry for this Korean kid, Jin just walked right by like everyone else.

Over the next several weeks, this incident really bothered him. He couldn't get these questions out of his mind:

"Why didn't I DO something?"
"Why am I such a coward?"
"How could I just walk by without even saying a word?"
"WHAT IS WRONG WITH ME????"
"And I'm supposed to be a Christian! God must be so ashamed of me!"

The more he thought about it, the more depressed he got. He continued to blame himself, and in feeling worthless he started to skip school and church.

Questions

1. How do you feel about Jin? Do you blame him for walking by the bullied kid without helping him? Can you empathize with Jin?

2. What do you think about the guilt Jin felt afterward? Do you think this was a healthy/productive way to respond to what had happened? Why or why not?

Summary

We all sin and make mistakes. Jin recognized that it was wrong for him not to have reached out to the bullied kid, and regretted not helping him at his time of need. But when Jin engaged in continual self-accusation and blame, he spiraled down into self-hatred. When we sin, we are called to express contrition and turn toward God for forgiveness and healing. If we get stuck in regret and accumulate guilt without moving beyond to seek forgiveness from God, we are in danger of being imprisoned in a cycle of self-accusation and self-hatred that can lead to problems like eating disorder or depression.

Text

Psalm 40:1-3

1 I waited patiently for the LORD;
he turned to me and heard my cry.
2 He lifted me out of the slimy pit,
out of the mud and mire;
he set my feet on a rock
and gave me a firm place to stand.
3 He put a new song in my mouth,
a hymn of praise to our God.
Many will see and fear the LORD
and put their trust in him.

Philippians 4:6-7

6 Do not be anxious about anything, but in every situation, by prayer and petition, with thanksgiving, present your requests to God. 7 And the peace of God, which transcends all understanding, will guard your hearts and your minds in Christ Jesus.

Questions

1. Name two images in the psalm that describe Jin's situation. What are these images and how do they describe Jin's struggle with self-blame?

2. Why does the writer of the psalm offer a hymn of praise (v. 3)? How does God deliver us from the slimy pit and put us on a firm place? What does the Bible say about it?

Application

Philippians 4:6-7 is another text that emphasizes how God will deliver us from crippling anxiety. These two verses can be easily memorized and can help us claim God's promise that when we present our anxieties, burdens and requests to God by prayer and petition with thanksgiving, the peace of God that surpasses all understanding will guard our hearts and minds in Christ Jesus. Let us memorize these verses this week and claim God's promise of peace and shalom for us.

LESSON 10

"Insider, Outsider"

Story

Helen is a Korean American in her mid-twenties, working as a newspaper editor in New York City. While walking to her office building with her Indian co-worker, Priya, some men sitting on the sidewalk began to shout at Priya, "*Go back to your country, terrorist! God hates Muslims!*" Helen couldn't believe what she just heard and retorted back to the men, "*She is Hindu, not Muslim! Don't be ignorant racists!*" Helen gave a hard look at the men and continued to walk quickly with Priya to their office building. When they got to the office, Priya thanked Helen for standing up and defending her.

This whole incident reminded Helen of her childhood, which she spent in a predominantly white suburb in Ohio. She could not forget the painful memory of being bullied as the only Asian-American in her class. Her classmates would pull at the outer corners of their eyes until they resembled slits. They would say things like, "*Ching chong ling long!*" and ask her to interpret their words. Even when she was in high school and won accolades for her high school newspaper articles, there were constant reminders that she wasn't a "real" American like the rest of her Caucasian classmates. They would ask her, "*Where are you from?*" or "*Where did you learn to speak English?*" Helen knew that they asked these questions innocently, but they made her feel like an outsider. Despite having been born and raised in the United States, Helen felt like a foreigner who would be forever defined and judged by her Asian facial features.

Questions

1. What are some of the ways in which Helen and Priya experienced discrimination and bullying?

2. In your opinion, why do people bully or discriminate others? What is the impact of discrimination and bullying on the victims?

Summary

Experiences of discrimination and bullying are all too common for Asian North Americans, as Helen and Priya's experiences demonstrate. Many times, victims of discrimination and bullying remain silent victims rather than finding the courage to stand up against injustice. Other times, the victims also become perpetrators of the same evil to others who may be different from them. It is important to recognize that our words and actions are extremely powerful and can be used to either uplift or destroy. Students need to learn to confront the evils as well as repent of the ways that they themselves may have hurt others different from them in the past (i.e., based on religious orientation, sexual orientation, disability, physical appearance, etc.). Instead of fearing, teasing, or ostracizing people who are "different," we need to show love for them just as God showed love for us.

Text

Leviticus 19:33-34 (ESV)

[33] "When a stranger sojourns with you in your land, you shall not do him
wrong. [34] You shall treat the stranger who sojourns with you as the native
among you, and you shall love him as yourself, for you were strangers in
the land of Egypt: I am the LORD your God.

1 Peter 2:10 (ESV)

[10] Once you were not a people, but now you are God's people; once you
had not received mercy, but now you have received mercy.

Questions

1. How did God want the Israelites to treat people who were different from themselves? According to the text why should Israelites demonstrate hospitality toward outsiders?

2. Why is it important for us as Christians to stand up for "strangers" in our midst?

Application

How can we show the love of Christ toward those who feel like "outsiders"? Name three specific things you can do.

LESSON 11

"Parents Over Me = Love^2"

Story

Tracy and her mother are extremely close, but this was not always so. She remembers the time she had her first conflict with her mother. She was nine years old, her parents were getting divorced, and her mother was moving her across the country to a new school, new friends, and basically a new life. On the day they moved into their new apartment, Tracy's mother was stressed and busy settling in, unpacking boxes, and asked if Tracy could find a blanket in the bottom drawer of the dresser in her mother's room. Tracy could not find it, even though she searched hard for a good five minutes. When she told her mom that there was no such item, her mother got furious and stormed into the bedroom, yelling at Tracy about why she couldn't even help her mother with the smallest things. Well, her mother also couldn't find the blanket but did end up finding it in the drawer *above*. Tracy looked at her mom smugly, waiting for an apology from her, that her mom made the mistake and unjustly yelled at Tracy. Instead, Tracy's mom proceeded to scream at her more that she couldn't do anything right and how unhelpful she was and should have thought to look in the drawer above! Tracy was livid, to say the least. The nerve of her mother! Here she was, only nine years old, moved across the country away from her home, her family, her friends, running around trying to be helpful in any way she could, and all her mom could do was yell at her?? Tracy yelled back at her mom and they got into a very big argument, and of course Tracy was the one who got in trouble and punished for the entire incident. It was the start of a very bad period in their relationship.

Questions

1. After reading Tracy's story, were you angry for her? Did it seem fair how her mother reacted to Tracy? In what way might you understand what Tracy is going through?

2. Share a time when you got into an argument with your parents because you thought they were treating you unfairly.

Summary

Oftentimes what seems like a completely unfair situation actually turns out to be something we didn't expect. In times of conflict with our parents, we automatically think, "*Why are they yelling at me?? Why are they so upset with me, since I didn't do anything wrong?!*" In these moments, we need to stop and reflect on why our parents are doing or saying these things. Many times there is a bigger issue at hand.

Text

Philippians 2:1-11

1 Therefore if you have any encouragement from being united with Christ,
if any comfort from his love, if any common sharing in the Spirit, if any
tenderness and compassion, 2 then make my joy complete by being like-
minded, having the same love, being one in spirit and of one mind. 3 Do
nothing out of selfish ambition or vain conceit. Rather, in humility value
others above yourselves, 4 not looking to your own interests but each of
you to the interests of the others.
5 In your relationships with one another, have the same mindset as Christ
Jesus:

> *6 Who, being in very nature God,*
> *did not consider equality with God something to be used to his own advantage;*
> *7 rather, he made himself nothing*
> *by taking the very nature of a servant,*
> *being made in human likeness.*
> *8 And being found in appearance as a man,*
> *he humbled himself*
> *by becoming obedient to death—*
> *even death on a cross!*
> *9 Therefore God exalted him to the highest place*
> *and gave him the name that is above every name,*
> *10 that at the name of Jesus every knee should bow,*
> *in heaven and on earth and under the earth,*
> *11 and every tongue acknowledge that Jesus Christ is Lord,*
> *to the glory of God the Father.*

Questions

1. According to Philippians 2:1-11, how would you describe the mindset of Jesus Christ?

2. In light of the mindset of Jesus that you described above, what would it look like in your relationship with your parents?

Application

Think about the situations in your parents' lives (e.g., work, lack of sleep, money problems, etc.). Choose one thing you can do this week that would reflect the mindset of Jesus Christ.

LESSON 12

"Lost in Translation"

Story

Larry's Story

My parents were in the restaurant business for as long as I can remember. My mom owned the place, so she was out at dawn and home near bedtime. My dad was an interrogator for the army, so he was hardly home. I grew up pretty much alone. When I was in 6th grade, my dad was sent out of the country for a four-year assignment. Since no one was ever home, I started acting out and ditching classes. I remember my mom yelling at me and asking me why I was behaving this way. I yelled back at her to mind her own business—she was never around anyway. Why did she care now? She told me that she loved me. Didn't I see her working so hard to provide for me? I told her that this wasn't love.

When high school rolled around, it just got worse. The school contacted my mom with an expulsion notice—I had missed over 52 days of school. This news came the day after my dad finally came back. This was the first time I saw my father cry. He hadn't even cried when his mother passed away. He was a tough man, but he broke down on my account. It wasn't until then that I realized how much my parents loved me. Providing for me, working hard—all of it was to show how much they cared. Starting over at a new school is going to be hard, but things have changed for me.

Questions

1. What makes Larry feel so frustrated in the story? In what ways can you identify with his frustration? Are there any differences between how love is understood and expressed between you and your parents?

2. Why do you think Larry's father cried? If the father were able to articulate how he was feeling in that moment, what do you think he would say?

3. If you were Larry, how would you communicate his frustrations and feelings to his parents?

Summary

Korean culture tends to place great value on acts of service—task and achievement. Consequently, Korean immigrant parents often express love to their children by working hard, long hours to provide money and resources.

The Story of David and Absalom

David had many sons from many wives and concubines, which was the custom of a king at that time. Absalom was the third son of David, and he had a lovely full sister, Tamar. The tragic conflict between David and Absalom began when Amnon, Absalom's half-brother, lusted for Tamar and raped her; but David did not take any punitive action against Amnon. Outraged about injustice, Absalom waited silently for two years, and finally had Amnon killed. Right after his assassination, Absalom fled and was in exile beyond the Jordan River for three years. Even after he was allowed by David to return Jerusalem, Absalom began to lay a plot to topple his father; he stealthily "stole the hearts of the people of Israel" (2 Samuel 15:6) with faked humility and promise of justice for all. Four years later, Absalom, now with strong military and surging popularity among the people of Israel and Judah, declared himself to be the new king in Hebron. He raped David's concubines and attacked Jerusalem, forcing David to flee from Jerusalem. Eventually the mortal battle was about to take place between David's and Absalom's forces in the forest of Ephraim. Even then David ordered his captains, "Be gentle with the young man Absalom for my sake," (2 Samuel 18:5). Our text opens with the story of a Cushite reporting the result of the mortal battle.

Unfortunately, the standard for love in American culture emphasizes the need for emotional engagement and affirmation. There is a definite disconnect there, but while our Korean parents may not be as good as we would like them to be with their words, both expressions of love are valid. Additionally, while our parents may not be perfect, they still love us. Jesus calls us to love them.

Text

2 Samuel 18:31-33

31 Then the Cushite arrived and said, "My lord the king, hear the good news! The LORD has vindicated you today by delivering you from the hand of all who rose up against you."
32 The king asked the Cushite, "Is the young man Absalom safe?"
The Cushite replied, "May the enemies of my lord the king and all who rise up to harm you be like that young man."
33 The king was shaken. He went up to the room over the gateway and wept. As he went, he said: "O my son Absalom! My son, my son Absalom! If only I had died instead of you—O Absalom, my son, my son!"

Questions

1. Contrary to the expectation of his soldiers and advisers, David did not rejoice at the death of Absalom but rather bitterly wept over it even though Absalom had tried to kill him. Why do you think David wept?

2. What can we learn about the love of the parents from the story? What similarity do you see between David and Larry's father?

Application

Write and share some practical ways in which you can show your love to your parents this week.

If you are feeling adventurous, map out the rest of the year and commit to one tangible act of love per month for your parents! Ask your Bible Study group and teacher to keep you accountable!

LESSON 13

"God's Amazing Love"

Story

Charlie grew up in Texas in a Korean home. Even as a little kid, he loved cars. As soon as Charlie turned sixteen he went to the DMV and got his learner's permit. He could not wait to drive. But when his father started to teach him to drive, it was not good. Charlie wanted to practice in their new car, a fully loaded Black Acura SUV with all the electronic bells and whistles. But Charlie's father loved that car and wouldn't let Charlie touch it. He wouldn't even let Charlie's mother drive that car. Instead, he took Charlie out in their 15-year-old beat up Chevy. It was embarrassing for Charlie to be seen in that car and driving with his father was no picnic. Charlie's father was so tense when Charlie was behind the wheel that whenever he wanted Charlie to brake, he would scream in Korean, "*Breakie, breakie*!!!!!" This drove Charlie crazy. He wished he could drive by himself.

One weekend, while his father was on a business trip, Charlie took the keys to the Acura. He planned to take it out for a quick spin, just ten minutes...just to get the feel of it. No one would know. He didn't make it out of the driveway. As he backed out a pickup truck rammed into the side of the car. All the airbags exploded. The car was totaled and Charlie suffered pretty severe whiplash. He was taken to the hospital, treated and released. The doctor ordered Charlie a few days of bed rest. Charlie's mother was worried that he might be more hurt than he seemed. But that wasn't what worried Charlie. Charlie knew he would be toast when his father returned. It worried him so much that he couldn't sleep. The next day Charlie heard his father come in the house and up the stairs to his room. Charlie was terrified. He turned as white as a ghost when he saw his father's face. "I'm so sorry Dad! It was all my fault. I'm so sorry!"

Ending #1

His father strode over to the bed and smacked Charlie on the head, yelling, "You ungrateful little brat! You disobeyed me and destroyed my car! You are going to pay for what you did! You are never driving again!" He fumed with anger. Fearful, Charlie just curled up in his bed crying.

Ending #2

His father rushed to Charlie's side. With tears in his eyes, he grasped Charlie's hand and said, "Son, I was so worried that you were hurt...or even worse. Thank God you are okay. Thank God!"

Charlie was confused. He had been expecting his father to be furious. He had been steeling himself for lots of yelling, maybe even a whack on the head. Charlie said, "But dad, the car... it was totaled..."

Charlie's father interrupted, "Yes, I loved that car... But I love you more. Cars can be replaced. You can't." With that, he embraced his son and they both cried in relief."

Questions

1. Which ending is more realistic? Which ending do you like better and why?

2. Describe how each ending characterizes Charlie's relationship with his father.

3. Assuming that this story is about our image/understanding of God, which ending describes how you understand God? Do you see God as an angry father who is ready to punish you for what you have done wrong? Or do you see God as a loving and forgiving father? Why?

Summary

This story provides two different ways of thinking about God through the two different endings. Is God a moral accountant who keeps exact records of all of our thoughts and deeds? Is He eager to punish us when we sin? Or is God like the loving and merciful father who not only forgave Charlie, but also embraced him with love?

Text

Psalm 103:8-12

8 The LORD is compassionate and gracious,
slow to anger, abounding in love.
9 He will not always accuse,
nor will he harbor his anger forever;
10 he does not treat us as our sins deserve
or repay us according to our iniquities.
11 For as high as the heavens are above the earth,
so great is his love for those who fear him;
12 as far as the east is from the west,
so far has he removed our transgressions from us.

1 John 1:9

9 If we confess our sins, he is faithful and just and will forgive us our sins and purify us from all unrighteousness.

Questions

1. How does the first text in Psalms describe God? What kind of God is this? Is this God approachable?

2. How does the second passage in 1 John describe God? Would you be willing to come before this kind of God and confess your sins before Him?

Application

1. Memorize 1 John 1:9 and claim it as God's promise for you. When we confess our sins to God, there is nothing that can separate us from Him.

2. Share with the group a time when someone forgave you. What was that experience like?

14 LESSON

"We Are NOT What We Wear"

Story

Karen eyed the girl at the mall. *"Coach bag. Whatever,"* Karen thought. She tightened her grip on the Louis Vuitton bag she was carrying over her left shoulder and brushed past the girl. Karen loved the way her fancy purses and clothes made her feel. She even got a part time job at the make up counter at Nordstrom, so she could get discounts and have money to buy the brand name items she saw the fashion bloggers are using. Her mom would also chip in to help her to buy the bags, even though they struggled to make ends meet with her father's dry cleaning business. Karen sometimes wondered if she should feel bad about it, but having those things made her feel good about herself and better than others. Maybe some girls at school are athletic or smart, but Karen laughed when she saw them shopping at cheap stores.

"Whatever. I am different from them. No one can match the clothes and accessories that I have," she thought.

Questions

1. Why do you think Karen likes fancy purses and clothing?

2. What do you think Karen would feel about herself if she didn't have those things?

Summary

The desire to feel affirmed and accepted by others is a strong drive in all of us. It is part of human nature. And today fancy clothing, an expensive car, and a big house have become status symbols by which many people try to define who they are. Even Christians today feel the pressure to conform to this trend under the heavy influence of commercial media. However, material goods and brand name fashions cannot define our true value as a person. Although it is important to satisfy our basic needs of food, shelter, clothes, education, jobs, and such, we should not let our material possessions define who we are. Furthermore, it should be noted that excessive consumption often results in financial difficulty, not to mention the environmental damage due to overburdening of our planet with waste.

Text

Matthew 6:25-34

25 "Therefore I tell you, do not worry about your life, what you will eat or
drink; or about your body, what you will wear. Is not life more than food,
and the body more than clothes? 26 Look at the birds of the air; they do
not sow or reap or store away in barns, and yet your heavenly Father feeds
them. Are you not much more valuable than they? 27 Can any one of you
by worrying add a single hour to your life?
28 "And why do you worry about clothes? See how the flowers of the field
grow. They do not labor or spin. 29 Yet I tell you that not even Solomon in
all his splendor was dressed like one of these. 30 If that is how God clothes
the grass of the field, which is here today and tomorrow is thrown into
the fire, will he not much more clothe you—you of little faith? 31 So do not
worry, saying, 'What shall we eat?' or 'What shall we drink?' or 'What shall
we wear?' 32 For the pagans run after all these things, and your heavenly
Father knows that you need them. 33 But seek first his kingdom and his
righteousness, and all these things will be given to you as well. 34 Therefore
do not worry about tomorrow, for tomorrow will worry about itself. Each
day has enough trouble of its own.

Questions

1. What does Jesus mean when he says that life is more than food and the body more than clothes (v. 25)?

2. In verse 32, Jesus says, "*For the pagans run after all these things.*" What does he mean by this statement, and how does it apply to Karen's obsession with fashion and fads?

Application

1. Think about your monthly allowance and your spending habits. How much of it do you spend on clothing, purses, sporting goods, video games, cosmetics, and other perfume, gadgets, etc.? Which of them are really necessary and which are not? In light of this lesson, name one change that you are willing to make on how you spend your money. Come and share your experience in your next meeting together.

2. List some things that are more important in your life than fashion, fads, and gigs.

LESSON 15

"Day by Day"

Story

It felt like Jane's world was falling apart. At school, she was struggling to make friends. There was always the feeling of inadequacy: not being pretty enough to be popular or smart enough to be proud of. When she looked around, it seemed like everyone was better and happier than she was. She felt that she was inadequate. So Jane tried to prove herself in her studies. Her parents kept telling her that good grades would lead to a bright future with a great paying job and a wonderful family. She tried hard and her grades improved, but even her improved grades were not good enough to satisfy her parents and their dreams for her of an Ivy League degree. Jane has gotten frustrated and anxious, wondering whether she could ever be good enough. She even questioned whether she should continue her responsibility as president of her youth group. "*What good is this position for me when I am struggling,*" she asked herself.

Jane's teacher at church encouraged her to trust God and find peace in God. But Jane felt too inadequate for God who is perfect and in control of everything. She could not cast off the doubt whether God really cares for a person like her. She thought to herself, "*Maybe if my grades improve further, I could begin to trust God.*"

Questions

1. In what ways can you relate to Jane's story? Please elaborate.

2. Why do you think Jane is having difficulty in trusting God with her life? How does her view of God influence her ability to trust God?

Summary

Many think that God is the last resort to solving our problems when all other means and methods are exhausted. Or God is needed when we die in order to go to heaven. But God doesn't want to be an insurance policy that we put away until we are in a desperate situation. As the Spirit, God is everywhere and God wants to be part of our daily life as our Friend in good times as well as bad times. Amazingly, God really does care about even our most mundane stuff!

Text

Genesis: 15:1-6

1 *After this, the word of the LORD came to Abram in a vision:*

"Do not be afraid, Abram.
I am your shield,
your very great reward."
2 But Abram said, "Sovereign LORD, what can you give me since I remain
childless and the one who will inherit my estate is Eliezer of Damascus?"
3 And Abram said, "You have given me no children; so a servant in my
household will be my heir."
4 Then the word of the LORD came to him: "This man will not be your heir,
but a son who is your own flesh and blood will be your heir." 5 He took him
outside and said, "Look up at the sky and count the stars—if indeed you
can count them." Then he said to him, "So shall your offspring be."
6 Abram believed the LORD, and he credited it to him as righteousness.

Proverbs 16:1, 3

1 To humans belong the plans of the heart,
but from the LORD comes the proper answer of the tongue.

3 Commit to the LORD whatever you do,
and he will establish your plans.

Questions

1. This was not the first time God told Abram of His promise to bless him with children (Gen. 13:16). So why was Abram still worried and anxious in this text?

2. How did Abram show his trust in God after he heard God's reassuring words?

Application

1. Barrenness was an area in which Abram had difficulty in trusting God. Lis a few things you are having difficulty in trusting God with. Share with your group.

2. Trusting God is born out of our ongoing relationship with Him as we walk daily with Him. This means that we are to have daily fellowship with God through prayer, meditation, reading of scripture, and participation in church life. In light of this understanding, how would you describe your daily fellowship with God? Do you feel the presence of God regularly? If not, what will you do about it?

LESSON 16
"Unconditional"

Story

"Mom, Dad, I want to go to a Christian college and study music so I can fully develop my talent, and then use it in missions," Jessica said.

"No. God made you smart enough to be a really good doctor. Music is a hobby that you can do any time. You can become a doctor and then do medical missions all you want when you're older and successful. Since you love helping people, do it by going to medical school. You're not going to a Bible school. You're going to go to a university that can give higher degrees."

"I don't want to go to medical school! Who cares if I'm rich, if I'm not going to be happy!? I'm trying to obey God, and you're not letting me!!" Jessica yelled in frustration. Becoming some rich doctor seemed superficial and materialistic to her. After all, she knew success was not measured by how much money one made.

"Jessica, it's not just about the money or title. We say this *because* we love you."

[story to be continued]

Questions

1. If you were Jessica, would you have a difficult time honoring your parents in this situation? Explain.

2. Can you point out the wisdom in what her parents are saying? How can you tell they are truly saying it out of love?

Summary

When someone disapproves of our passions or convictions, it usually becomes difficult to take in anything they are saying. Jessica's growing frustration towards her parents began to close the door of her ears and heart. Fortunately for Jessica, her mother explained clearly why they disapproved of Jessica's plans.

[story continued]

After a long pause, her mother responded, "Jessica, we don't care if you are rich or famous.

Money is not everything. Especially when it becomes an idol—it ruins people. But the more you have, the more you can be *generous* in giving to those in need. You won't have to stress and struggle to get by, and you'll be able to bless others *joyfully.* We want you to be successful because you'll be able to serve God better."

Summary

Hearing this from her mother made it easier for Jessica to honor her parents. In the end, Jessica did not follow their exact wishes, but she honored them wholeheartedly. *How can that be*, you ask? Let's explore the Scriptures to understand what it means to honor someone.

Relevant Definitions of HONOR

English (Merriam-Webster Dictionary)

To show appreciation, respect, or affection for (someone) with a public celebration.

Hebrew *kabed* (כבד)

To be heavy or weighty; to honor, esteem, or consider competent (in something).

Greek *timao* (τιμάω)

To set a price on; to value, prize, show high regard for; to attribute high status to someone; honor and revere

Text

Deuteronomy 5:16

16 *"Honor your father and your mother, as the LORD your God has commanded you, so that you may live long and that it may go well with you in the land the LORD your God is giving you."*

Ephesians 6:2-3

2 *"Honor your father and mother"—which is the first commandment with a promise—* 3 *"so that it may go well with you and that you may enjoy long life on the earth."*

Questions

1. According to the texts, why should we honor our parents? Should we honor them even if they are not good and honorable (for reasons other than the blessing that is promised to those who honor their parents)?

2. Given the definitions of "honor" in the side box, recommend at least one honoring response (word and/or action) that Jessica could give to her parents.

Application

Note that honoring is "giving/placing weight" to something or someone. In this understanding, honoring is as much about our inner attitude as it is about our actions. Name one thing that you will do this week that would be honoring your parents.

17 LESSON

"Absent God"

Story

Debbie beat her fists on the floor as she cried uncontrollably. Her parents had just told her that they were getting a divorce and she was so angry. Ever since her dad moved out of the house, Debbie had been praying and praying that her parents would stop fighting and get back together. *"I prayed so hard!"* Debbie sobbed angrily. *"Is God even real?"* Debbie wasn't sure she could even believe in God anymore since she wasn't sure He was real. Her youth pastor had just given a sermon on how Christians should trust and believe in God. How could she have faith now that God hadn't answered her prayers? Was she a bad Christian? Debbie didn't know how much more she could take.

Questions

1. Is it okay for Debbie to have doubts about God? Why or why not?

2. What would you say if Debbie asked you why God didn't answer her prayer?

Summary

Like Debbie, most of us have probably experienced times when God has seemed absent or silent. It is natural during these times to wonder where God is, or even to doubt if God is really present. At the same time, these doubts can be difficult to talk about in the church, where we are expected to simply trust and believe in God. Yet the Bible is very honest about our human experience of doubt. It does not hide the fact that God sometimes feels very absent. In the Bible, doubt is not the opposite of faith. In fact, wrestling with doubt can be a critical stepping stone toward deeper faith.

Text

Psalm 13 (ESV)

To the choirmaster. A Psalm of David.

1 *How long, O Lord? Will you forget me forever?*
How long will you hide your face from me?
2 *How long must I take counsel in my soul*

and have sorrow in my heart all the day?
How long shall my enemy be exalted over me?
3 *Consider and answer me, O LORD my God;*
light up my eyes, lest I sleep the sleep of death,
4 *lest my enemy say, "I have prevailed over him,"*
lest my foes rejoice because I am shaken.
5 *But I have trusted in your steadfast love;*
my heart shall rejoice in your salvation.
6 *I will sing to the LORD,*
because he has dealt bountifully with me.

Questions

1. What feelings are being expressed by David in verses 1-4? Does it surprise you to find such feelings in a prayer to God? Why or why not?

2. How does the tone of the psalm shift in verses 5-6? What feelings are being expressed in these verses?

3. In verses 5-6, what does David decide to put his trust and his hope in? Why do you think David continues to trust even when he feels abandoned and ignored?

Food for Thought

"Faith is deliberate confidence in the character of God whose ways you may not understand at the time."

~Oswald Chambers

David's faith is founded on his trust in the "character of God." He had already experienced God's goodness, and knew that God loved him with "steadfast love."

Application

1. Think about Debbie's situation one more time. After reading Psalm 13, do you think it is okay for Debbie to have doubts and to be angry? What could you say to someone like Debbie who is struggling with doubting God?

2. Was there a time in your life when you struggled with your faith? How did you cope with it? Share with your group.

LESSON 18

"What Would Jesus Post?"

Story

Jinsung sat at the cafeteria table laughing with his friends as they watched a YouTube post on their Facebook of U.S. soldiers in Afghanistan imitating American cheerleaders who covered a pop song. Danny exclaimed, "Dude! My cousin's in Iraq right now, I bet he'd like this! I'm gonna re-post it."

Someone joked, "Sure... it's for your 'cousin.' Just admit it. You wanna re-post it because there's hot girls in it!"

When Jinsung went home and sat in front of his Facebook, he thought about the funny video he saw earlier that day, and was considering re-posting it to his wall. While he was searching for it, he came across a video of his favorite song from the new Hillsong album. He paused for a moment, and considered which he should post as a highlight for the day: the Soldiers or Hillsong. He went with Hillsong because he thought it would be a more uplifting post. Within seconds, a few girls from Jinsung's youth group "liked" the song and commented things like, "*Jin! That's exactly what I needed to hear today. It cheered me up. Thx for sharing*!" and "*Nice bro. Like ur taste in music!*" and "*singing along right now.*"

Encouraging words like that made Jinsung feel good about his choice to re-post an edifying video and he thought to himself, "*I wonder which song I could share with my fans next week? Maybe I could find a cool Bible verse to go along with it, too! Man, Sarah jundosanim would be so proud of me. Ooh, I should show it to her and ask her to buy me some patbingsoo!*"

Questions

1. What do you think of Jinsung's decision to repost the Hillsong video rather than the American soldiers' video?

2. How did Jinsung's posting of the Hillsong video on his Facebook page help his friends?

Summary

As rapid technological advances present us with new ways of connecting, communicating, and building relationships, we have both the freedom and responsibility to make wise decisions on its use. These new capabilities influence us and others. It's important to reflect on how will we use our influence—to serve and glorify ourselves, or serve and glorify God, thereby ultimately, serve and bless others. In this story, a group of teenage boys interact with social media and watch a video, and we saw how two friends make two different decisions about how to respond using social media. Let's see what the Word of God has to say about how we make decisions and how they affect others.

Text

1 Corinthians 10:23-24; 10:31-11:1

23 "I have the right to do anything," you say—but not everything is benefi-
cial. "I have the right to do anything"—but not everything is constructive.
24 No one should seek their own good, but the good of others.

31 So whether you eat or drink or whatever you do, do it all for the glory
of God. 32 Do not cause anyone to stumble, whether Jews, Greeks or the
church of God— 33 even as I try to please everyone in every way. For I
am not seeking my own good but the good of many, so that they may be
saved.
11:1 Follow my example, as I follow the example of Christ.

Questions

1. How is Paul's understanding of the "right" ("I have the right to do anything") different from how we normally view it in our culture?

2. Re-read 1 Corinthians 10:23-24 in the NIV and CEB versions:

> *23 Everything is permitted, but everything isn't beneficial.*
> *Everything is permitted, but everything doesn't build others*
> *up. 24 No one should look out for their own advantage, but*
> *they should look out for each other.* (CEB)

Why do you think Apostle Paul differentiates between things being "permissible" and things being "beneficial" and "constructive"?

Application

Log onto your Facebook page (or another social networks). Review all your posts in the last week. What are some of the things that you think are beneficial and helpful for viewers and what are just permissible (e.g., entertaining) but not beneficial? List them and share.

LESSON 19

“Road to Reconciliation”

Story

Elizabeth's Story

Most of my life, I grew up with a very low opinion of myself. People always compared me with my sister, and whether it was a positive or negative difference, I always took it negatively. Slowly, hatred began to grow. I struggled to find my identity for a very long time. It was hard to really believe that God loved *me* because somehow I was convinced that I had to be like my sister, but I wasn't. We started competing with each other, and our mutual resentment began to grow. We rarely talked to each other.

I was hungry for more of God's love, yet I didn't know what to do about how I had been feeling. Months later at a church retreat, my pastor prayed for me. She told me that God could give us freedom from our hurts through sharing and reconciliation. I had been growing closer to a few girls at church, so I decided to give it a try. As I shared with them, I was encouraged to make up with my sister.

After the retreat, I wrote my sister a letter expressing my feelings of hurts and resentment, as well as my love for her and desire to mend the relationship. I was nervous about how she would respond to my letter. To my surprise, she wrote back expressing her understanding, and desire for reconciliation with me. We apologized and forgave each other.

Questions

1. In what ways do you relate to Elizabeth's struggles and to her story? Is there someone in your life that you want to or need to reconcile with?

2. What do you think gave Elizabeth the courage to seek reconciliation with her sister?

Summary

Seeking reconciliation by sharing one's deep feelings can be extremely scary. It can be even more daunting for us because of our Korean culture, which is "shame-based." It discourages the honest sharing of feelings, so personal struggles and sins are usually kept hidden. It is not surprising that sharing our brokenness to one another is not something that we naturally do, but sometimes, the strength and support of our community and friends are what we need to face something as difficult and counterintuitive as forgiveness!

Text

Genesis 50: 15-21

15 When Joseph's brothers saw that their father was dead, they said,
"What if Joseph holds a grudge against us and pays us back for all the
wrongs we did to him?" 16 So they sent word to Joseph, saying, "Your
father left these instructions before he died: 17 'This is what you are to
say to Joseph: I ask you to forgive your brothers the sins and the wrongs
they committed in treating you so badly.' Now please forgive the sins of
the servants of the God of your father." When their message came to him,
Joseph wept.
18 His brothers then came and threw themselves down before him. "We
are your slaves," they said.
19 But Joseph said to them, "Don't be afraid. Am I in the place of God?
20 You intended to harm me, but God intended it for good to accomplish
what is now being done, the saving of many lives. 21 So then, don't be
afraid. I will provide for you and your children." And he reassured them
and spoke kindly to them.

Joseph's Major Life Events

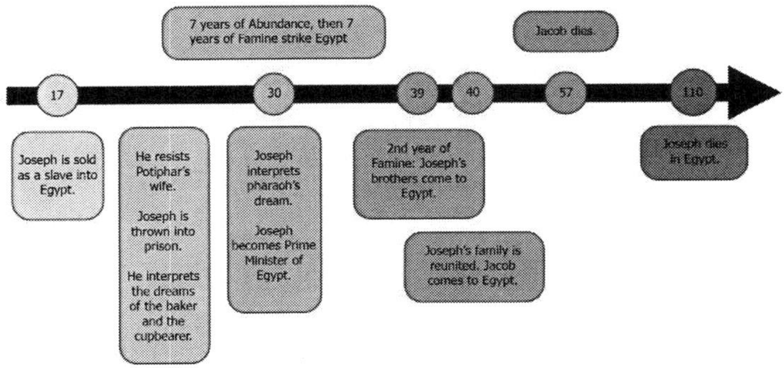

Questions

1. How do you think Joseph was able to forgive his brothers despite all that he went through?

2. What would have happened if Joseph had not forgiven his brothers? Give three examples of what might have happened.

Application

We have all been hurt or offended by someone, but we don't always get to go back in time or resolve it.

Write a letter to a person who has hurt or offended you in the past. Be sure to include in the letter what happened, how you were hurt or offended, how you felt, and your words of forgiveness now. Be sure to include a brief statement of how faith has allowed you to move from hurt to forgiveness.

20

LESSON

"What's Recycling Got To Do With God?"

Story

Peter just couldn't understand his friend Bridget, who was always bugging her high school about recycling and "saving the earth." I mean, he thought his friend was cool and all but always considered her as one of those hippie "tree huggers." Growing up, Peter was taught in Sunday school and currently in his youth group, how much God loved people... not trees! The message he got whenever he went to church was that God made EVERYTHING *for* mankind, and people are to consume and enjoy the abundance of God's creation. So, while Peter had been very involved with his church and serving in soup kitchens, he never gave a second thought about caring for the environment. That is, until John came to his youth group. John was different from his other Christian friends in the youth group. He seemed really fired up for God and helping the poor. Peter really liked that about John, but John also wanted to start up a recycling ministry in the youth group. He couldn't understand where John was coming from. "*Recycling program is for school, not for church,*" Peter thought.

One Friday night, while Peter was giving John a ride home after church, Peter jokingly asked him, "John, so how long have you been a tree hugger? C'mon, tell me the truth—if you had the choice of saving me or the tree, you'd save the tree, right?"

John quipped right back, "Was there even a doubt?"

After they both had a good laugh, John said, "But seriously, bro, God saved both according to the Bible. Take Noah's Ark for example. If God only cared about people, God could have just put Noah's family in the ark, but he wanted a pair of every living animal. Why?"

The question haunted Peter, and he decided that he would check out John's recycling ministry to find out more about what God has to do with recycling.

Questions

1. Who do you identify more with in the story—Peter or John? Why?

2. Do you think we have a responsibility as Christian to recycle? Why or Why not?

Summary

Many Korean North American churches do not consider creation care as an important part of their ministry. They usually focus on community, missions, and education, so it is not surprising that Peter did not see the importance of recycling as a Christian. It is not until John, a good Christian friend, starts a recycling program at his church that he starts to seriously consider why he, as a Christian, should be concerned about the earth.

Text

Genesis 9:8-17 (NRSV)

*8 Then God said to Noah and to his sons with him, 9 "As for me, I am
establishing my covenant with you and your descendants after you, 10 and
with every living creature that is with you, the birds, the domestic animals,
and every animal of the earth with you, as many as came out of the ark. 11
I establish my covenant with you, that never again shall all flesh be cut off
by the waters of a flood, and never again shall there be a flood to destroy
the earth." 12 God said, "This is the sign of the covenant that I make be-
tween me and you and every living creature that is with you, for all future
generations: 13 I have set my bow in the clouds, and it shall be a sign of
the covenant between me and the earth. 14 When I bring clouds over the
earth and the bow is seen in the clouds, 15 I will remember my covenant
that is between me and you and every living creature of all flesh; and the
waters shall never again become a flood to destroy all flesh. 16 When the
bow is in the clouds, I will see it and remember the everlasting covenant
between God and every living creature of all flesh that is on the earth." 17
God said to Noah, "This is the sign of the covenant that I have established
between me and all flesh that is on the earth."*

Questions

1. According to the passage, with whom does God make the covenant? Why do you think God included "every living creature" and "the earth" (v. 13) in the covenant?

2. What does this tell us about how we should treat "every living creature" on earth as well as the earth itself?

Food for Thought

True or False: Low-income neighborhoods have way more problems with asthma and allergies.

That's true. Can you guess why? Many of the gigantic oil, steel, and coal companies are located in poor neighborhoods. How do you think this happened? Why is this bad? What can be done about it?

Application

What are some ways in which you can care for the earth as a youth group?

21

LESSON

"Hey God, What's Your Name?"

Story

Jeremy's Story

My church youth group decided to focus on evangelism this month. So my youth pastor began a sermon series last week on the importance of sharing our faith with others and inviting others to Christ. The Friday night Bible Study last week also focused on the topic of evangelism and we were all encouraged to invite at least one friend to our church this month. I felt inspired and started to scan in my mind a person that I could invite to my church. After some searching, Young Ho came to my mind. "That's right! I can invite Young Ho to my church," I said to myself.

When I saw him in the school cafeteria a few days later, I took my tray and sat next to him. During our conversation together, I shared with him about my youth group and asked him if he would be interested in coming to my church the next Sunday.

Young Ho hesitated a little and said, "Mm... I don't know. I'll think about it." And then, after a short pause, he asked me, "Do you really believe in God? How do you know that God really exists?" He continued, "When I visited Sam's church last Christmas, I heard people talk about God's grace and God's Son as the light of the world. But I really didn't understand what they were talking about. Do you?"

I wanted to help Young Ho understand what he heard at the church and wanted to share with him about God. But when I tried to explain to him, I was surprised to find myself searching for words to describe God in a way that was clear and convincing to him. I did not know how to describe who God was in a personal way that others could relate to.

Questions

1. Can you relate with Jeremy in this story regarding the difficulty in describing his understanding of God in a personal way?

2. If you were Jeremy and were to describe to Young Ho your understanding of God, how would you explain who God is?

Summary

Sometimes, things that are most familiar to us can be the most difficult things to explain. Our understanding of God and our faith can be like this, especially if we have been a Christian for a long time. We may have heard about God so much that it makes sense in the church, but sound strange to those outside the church. So when we try to share our faith with non-believing friends, we may find it difficult to describe God in words that are concrete and easy to understand. One of the things that all growing Christians must learn is how to articulate their faith and God into their own words that are both personal and meaningful.

Text

Psalm 23

A Psalm of David.

1 The LORD is my shepherd, I shall not be in want.
2 He makes me lie down in green pastures, he leads me beside quiet waters,
3 he restores my soul. He guides me in paths of righteousness for his name's sake.
4 Even though I walk through the valley of the shadow of death, I will fear no evil, for you are with me; your rod and your staff, they comfort me.
5 You prepare a table before me in the presence of my enemies. You anoint my head with oil; my cup overflows.
6 Surely goodness and love will follow me all the days of my life, and I will dwell in the house of the LORD forever.

Questions

1. David used shepherding as a metaphor to describe God. Why is the fact that David was once a shepherd as a young boy important to note when one considers his choice of metaphor?

2. David could have said, "The Lord is a good shepherd." But, instead, he said, "The Lord is MY shepherd." Do you think adding the word "my" makes a huge difference in the meaning of this statement? Why or why not?

Application

1. David describes who God is to him by describing what a shepherd does. Describe three things that David portrays about God using the shepherd metaphor. (*Hint: An interpretation of Psalm is provided in a box below. Do not look until you give your answers.*)

Psalm 23

I shall not be in want. — *that's supply*
He makes me lie down in green pastures — *that's rest*
he leads me beside quiet waters — *that's refreshment*
he restores my soul — *that's healing*
He guides me in paths of righteousness — *that's guidance*
for his name's sakes — *that's purpose*
Even though I walk through the valley of the shadow of death, — *that's testing*
I will fear no evil, — *that's protection*
for you are with me; — *that's faithfulness*
your rod and your staff, they comfort me. — *that's discipline*
You prepare a table before me in the presence of my enemies. — *that's hope*
You anoint my head with oil; — *that's consecration*
my cup overflows. — *that's abundance*
Surely goodness and love will follow me all the days of my life, — *that's blessing*
and I will dwell in the house of the Lord — *that's security*
Forever. — *that's eternity*

And all of these begins with:

The Lord is my shepherd — *that's relationship*

2. What metaphor can you use from your own life to describe who God is to you? Write your version of Psalm 23. You may start by saying, "The Lord is my ___________"

22

LESSON

"Two Tales of Gender Identity: Girls Are...Boys Are..."

Story

Christie, Cindy, and Jennifer were hanging out at a coffee shop, talking about stuff. They were giggling because Christie had told them that her mother was determined to teach her to cook. "Oh my gosh, you guys, it was a disaster! My mom says I'll never get a nice Korean man to marry me if I can't learn to peel an apple properly."

Cindy snorted. "You? Cooking?!"

"I know, right? I told her that I wanted to go to college and get a job that makes lots of money. Then I'd pay someone else to cook for me!"

"Christie, *you're* the ideal husband!" Cindy exclaimed.

The girls laughed, but then Jennifer added, "My mom says guys will notice a girl who is sweet and pretty and quiet. She believes the guy should work hard and make all the money. Then be able to take care of our family."

"But we're so outgoing! Christie's president of the Key Club, and I play sports, and Jenny, you're a brainiac. Maybe that's just a Korean way of thinking, but not American like us!"

"My mom says that guys don't want to date girls who act like guys," Jennifer said.

"Well, I don't see why I should have to change," Christie tossed her hair. "People should like me the way I am."

Questions

1. Do you agree that all Korean North American women should act submissively, be quiet, and look pretty? Do you agree that all Korean North American men should be providers for the family, work hard, and be good at sports? Why or why not?

2. Can you think of people that you know personally (e.g., family, friends, relatives, teachers, etc.), who do not fit these gender stereotypes? How do these people help you to view male & female roles differently?

Summary

Girls and boys may feel pressured by the members of our community to conform to certain behaviors, and gender roles. These gender stereotypes have

significant cultural value and help people to identify their roles in society. Ye
we can sometimes feel limited by those roles.

Text

Judges 4:1-10

1 Again the Israelites did evil in the eyes of the Lord, now that Ehud was
dead. 2 So the Lord sold them into the hands of Jabin king of Canaan,
who reigned in Hazor. Sisera, the commander of his army, was based in
Harosheth Haggoyim. 3 Because he had nine hundred chariots fitted with
iron and had cruelly oppressed the Israelites for twenty years, they cried to
the Lord for help.
4 Now Deborah, a prophet, the wife of Lappidoth, was leading Israel at
that time. 5 She held court under the Palm of Deborah between Ramah
and Bethel in the hill country of Ephraim, and the Israelites went up to her
to have their disputes decided. 6 She sent for Barak son of Abinoam from
Kedesh in Naphtali and said to him, "The Lord, the God of Israel, com-
mands you: 'Go, take with you ten thousand men of Naphtali and Zebulun
and lead them up to Mount Tabor. 7 I will lead Sisera, the commander of
Jabin's army, with his chariots and his troops to the Kishon River and give
him into your hands.'"
8 Barak said to her, "If you go with me, I will go; but if you don't go with
me, I won't go."
9 "Certainly I will go with you," said Deborah. "But because of the course
you are taking, the honor will not be yours, for the Lord will deliver Sisera
into the hands of a woman." So Deborah went with Barak to Kedesh. 10
There Barak summoned Zebulun and Naphtali, and ten thousand men went
up under his command. Deborah also went up with him.

Questions

1. As you read the story of Deborah, is Deborah's position as a judge, proph-etess and leader surprising to you? Why or why not?

2. How does Deborah speak to Barak when she delivers her message? What does she say and how does Barak respond (vv. 6-8)? Do you think that Barak fits your idea of a typical male?

3. Do Deborah and Barak act in ways that surprise you? Why or why not?

Galatians 3:26-29

[26] So in Christ Jesus you are all children of God through faith, [27] for all of you who were baptized into Christ have clothed yourselves with Christ. [28] There is neither Jew nor Gentile, neither slave nor free, nor is there male andw female, for you are all one in Christ Jesus. [29] If you belong to Christ, then you are Abraham's seed, and heirs according to the promise.

Application

1. List three things that your family expects of you as a boy or a girl. Did this lesson help you to think about gender roles differently? If so how?

2. Name a person of opposite gender who has been a spiritual and moral inspiration to you. Share why.

23

LESSON

"Just One More"

Story

Megan flung her backpack down and walked briskly to her desk. *"Finally, the weekend,"* she thought to herself. After turning on the computer, she settled into her chair and tried to forget about the heavy load of schoolwork she had to finish over the weekend. Instead, she thought about the computer game she had just bought. She had had trouble concentrating in her classes because she was so caught up in strategizing for this game. It had taken her a mere three days to beat the last game she attempted. Perhaps if she started today, and played through the night, she could finish this one before going to church on Sunday. She would need to fuel up if she wanted to last through the night. Luckily, she had bought a six-pack of energy drinks on the way home. Megan closed the door so that her mom wouldn't barge in and disturb her. She knew her mom would be upset if she saw that Megan was playing yet another video game. At one point, Megan's mom had called her a "computer addict" and threatened to take her computer away. Megan had protested and said that she needed the computer to do her homework. *"Mom is so dramatic,"* thought Megan. *"So what if I do use the computer a lot? It's not like I'm looking at porn or anything."*

Questions

1. What is Megan's unhealthy compulsion (addiction)? How do you know?

2. Do you think Megan will ever find satisfaction in this compulsion? Why or why not?

3. If Megan were to continue on this path, what do you think would be the consequences in her life?

Summary

Megan has an unhealthy compulsion for playing computer games. There are many reasons why she may have this compulsion. Perhaps she seeks the companionship of online gamers like herself, or she likes the feeling of accomplishment that comes from beating others to advance a level. Whatever the reason, Megan's compulsion is unhealthy because it interferes with other areas of her life, including her academics, social circle, health, family, etc. Unhealthy compulsions and addictions are detrimental to our walk as Christians because they can be all-consuming and give us the illusion that we (not God) can satisfy our own needs, and ultimately take our time and energy away from building relationships with people.

Text

Isaiah 55:2

2 Why spend money on what is not bread, and your labor on what does not satisfy? Listen, listen to me, and eat what is good, and you will delight in the richest of fare.

Haggai 1:4-6

4 "Is it a time for you yourselves to be living in your paneled houses, while this house remains a ruin?"
5 Now this is what the LORD Almighty says: "Give careful thought to your
ways. 6 You have planted much, but harvested little. You eat, but never
have enough. You drink, but never have your fill. You put on clothes, but
are not warm. You earn wages, only to put them in a purse with holes in it."

Questions

1. How might these scripture passages be applied to addictions?

2. Can you think of an example of someone eating but not having enough or clothing oneself but not being warm?

Application

These are some common areas of addiction. Circle the one that you spend a lot of time in:

- Computer/Internet/Smartphone
- Food
- TV
- Shopping
- Sports
- Alcohol
- Tobacco
- Other: __________

C.S. Lewis defines addiction as "an ever-increasing craving for an ever diminishing pleasure."

24

LESSON

"Rallying for God's Righteousness"

Story

Angela woke up happily on Monday morning. Her school was having an assembly that she had organized through her student club to raise awareness for people in North Korea. As she got ready, Angela unfolded her shirt with a picture of the two Koreas on it, then she put it on. *"This is how I'm doing my part,"* she thought to herself.

Angela had become really interested in the topic of North Korea after a summer internship with a very well known organization that helps raise awareness for the suffering of the North Korean people. She remembered listening to the presentation about the starving people of the reclusive country, and the horrible ways in which they were treated and even killed. *"Those people are Korean, too,"* she had thought to herself, as she wondered why more people in South Korea didn't care about their sisters and brothers in North Korea.

After learning about Kenneth Bae, a Korean-American missionary who was imprisoned and sent to a concentration camp for sharing about God in North Korea, Angela decided to start a club at her school. Today was her chance to present everything she had learned to the whole school. She checked herself out in the mirror one more time before leaving. She felt proud.

Questions

1. Why do you think Angela felt proud of herself?

2. What was Angela's goal in organizing a school-wide assembly?

Summary

Christian service to God does not have to be always explicitly religious. Christian works for the poor, the widows, and the orphans are also considered ministry. There are many missionaries serving as teachers, nurses, and aid workers in some countries where evangelism is not permitted. Indeed, Jesus came to give life, and life abundantly. Whatever we do to help people to live with dignity is consistent with God's will. Angela's work to raise the people's awareness regarding the conditions in North Korea is also a kind of ministry.

Text

Psalm 10:12-18

12 Arise, LORD! Lift up your hand, O God.
Do not forget the helpless.
13 Why does the wicked man revile God?
Why does he say to himself,
"He won't call me to account"?
14 But you, God, see the trouble of the afflicted;
you consider their grief and take it in hand.
The victims commit themselves to you;
you are the helper of the fatherless.
15 Break the arm of the wicked man;
call the evildoer to account for his wickedness
that would not otherwise be found out.
16 The LORD is King for ever and ever;
the nations will perish from his land.
17 You, LORD, hear the desire of the afflicted;
you encourage them, and you listen to their cry,
18 defending the fatherless and the oppressed,
so that mere earthly mortals
will never again strike terror.

Questions

1. Why does the psalmist call on God's name and plead for God to "arise" in the face of rampant evils and injustices in a society?

2. How does the description of God's character portrayed in this Psalm differ from your traditional/common understanding of God? Name two or three major features highlighted in this Psalm.

3. Drawing from this Psalm, why do you think Christians should be compassionate and care about the helpless, the oppressed, and the afflicted around us?

Application

1. In what ways does your whole church engage in ministries of compassion and social justice? In what specific ways can your youth group engage in these ministries?

2. Have you ever interceded for people in North Korea? In light of Psalm 10, how would you pray for North Korea?

3. Choose one of the organizations listed below or find one from the Internet that interests you. Share about this organization with your group the next time you meet (i.e., what they do, whom they serve or help, how we can get involved, etc.).

List of social justice and community service organizations:

L.I.N.K. – Liberty in North Korea; http://libertyinnorthkorea.org
KCCD – Korean Churches for Community Development; http://www.kccd.org
KYCC – Koreatown Youth Community Center; http://www. kyccla.org
KRC – Korean Resource Center; http://www.krcla.org
KRCC – Korean American Resource Cultural Center; http://www.chicagokrcc.org; http://icirr.org/ko/content/korean-american-resource-and-cultural-center
NAKASEC – National Korean American Service & Education Consortium; http://nakasec.org/blog
APALC – Asian Pacific American Legal Center; www.advancingjustice-la.org
yKAN – Young Korean American Network; http://www.ykan.org
KACE – Korean American Civic Empowerment; http://www.kavc.org
KCSNY – The Korean Community Services of Metropolitan New York: http://www.kcsny.org

25

LESSON

"Stop Judging Me!"

Story

"Why don't you guys ever invite any of your friends to church?" Crystal's pastor was always trying to get them to bring more people to the youth group.

"We do!" Danny exclaimed.

"I mean on a normal Sunday... not just when we go ice skating or to Six Flags!"

Crystal laughed, but the truth was that she never felt comfortable asking her friends to come to church. She had a lot of great friends, but they didn't exactly fit the "good Christian" mold. And, to be honest, she was ok with that. They were good people, good friends. The last thing she wanted was to invite them to church where she knew they would feel judged. After all, that was part of why Crystal never felt comfortable sharing too deeply in her small group. Her family was the same. At church they always presented the image of the "good Korean Christian family," no matter what was really going on outside of church.

"*My life is my business,*" Crystal thought. "*I don't really want the others to know everything that's going on with me.*" With her other friends she could feel free to be herself, to not be judged. But not so with the people at church.

Questions

1. What do you think some of your friends would say or feel if you asked them about coming to church? Do you think they would worry about being judged? Why?

2. On a scale of 1 to 10, how comfortable would you feel sharing a personal struggle with: your pastor; your small group; your youth group; your church; or Jesus?

Summary

A recent study found that 87% of non-Christians felt that Christians were judgmental.[4] Many Christians probably feel the same way. We hear a lot about being loving and forgiving, and yet we often feel the opposite from our churches. We feel that we cannot open up and be ourselves because of how other people will think about us. Often we feel forced to hide our true struggles and our true lives in order to fit in. Yet, if we look at the stories

4 David Kinnaman, *unChristian* (Grand Rapids, MI: Baker Books 2007), 181.

that the Bible tells about Jesus, we find a very different picture. Jesus was the type of person you could be comfortable with.

Text

Matthew 9:9-13 (ESV)

9 As Jesus passed on from there, he saw a man called Matthew sitting at the tax booth, and he said to him, "Follow me." And he rose and followed him.
10 And as Jesus reclined at table in the house, behold, many tax collectors and sinners came and were reclining with Jesus and his disciples. 11 And when the Pharisees saw this, they said to his disciples, "Why does your teacher eat with tax collectors and sinners?" 12 But when he heard it, he said, "Those who are well have no need of a physician, but those who are sick. 13 Go and learn what this means, 'I desire mercy, and not sacrifice.' For I came not to call the righteous, but sinners."

Many people have a bad opinion of taxes and the IRS even today. But back in Jesus' time, it was even worse. For the Jews, tax collectors weren't just people who took your money for the government—they were thieves and traitors. Tax collectors, like Matthew in this story, often made their wealth by extortion and by demanding more money than was due. On top of that, they were representatives of the Roman government, the people most Jews considered their oppressors and enemies.

Questions

1. Given the reputation of tax collectors during the time of Jesus, how do you think the other disciples of Jesus responded when Jesus asked Matthew to follow him?

2. What is the difference between Jesus' attitude and the Pharisees' attitude toward Matthew?

Food for Thought

Imagine yourself as Matthew that day. You're sitting at that tax booth, starting another normal day. But today, Jesus came, called you by name, and asked you to follow Him.

Pretend you are writing a diary after you come home about your experience of hearing the call of Jesus. What would you say in your diary? Write a short journal entry and share it with each other.

Dear Diary,
...

Application

1. It is important to note that in the Bible passage, Jesus is not judgmental in the way the Pharisees are, but he clearly recognizes the sinfulness of Matthew and his friends, and desires for them to receive healing (v. 13). Do you think it is possible for us, like Jesus, to be loving and accepting of others while still being critical of the sin we see in their (and our) lives? How?

2. Are there any groups of people who you think feel especially judged by the church or by society? What are some concrete, practical things your youth group/church can do to be more welcoming to them and to others in general?

26

LESSON

"Psy or Sigh?"

Story

Jason feels Korean pride nowadays as he sees Psy perform on American TV shows. The non-Koreans at his high school constantly tell him how much they like Psy and how cool Koreans are. He often dances to "Gangnam Style" with his Korean as well as non-Korean friends, and has lots of fun doing it. However, some of his friends who go to the same high school and church sigh as they see him dance and sing the Gangnam Style with the crowd. They criticize him, saying that a Christian should avoid worldly culture. And they assert that there are anti-Christian messages in the song, which will damage his spiritual health. When he hears that, he just brushes off their criticism saying, "*It's just a song. I listen to it for fun. That's it. And the popular and fun song brings Korean pride, which is a very positive thing.*" At the same time, though he does not express it to anyone, he *does* wonder whether or not a song like that will affect his spiritual life. And, he even feels a little guilty for enjoying music like Gangnam Style more than Christian music.

Questions

1. If you were in Jason's shoes, how would you respond to the criticism of his church friends in the story?

2. Did the unprecedented success of Psy's Gangnam Style have any impact on your sense of identity as Korean North American Christians? Did it make you feel proud as Korean North American? What impact did it have on you as a Christian, if at all?

Summary

These days, many Korean North American youths are very proud of K-Pop. They carry the photos of K-pop stars and they share their videos with their friends regularly. It is a good thing to celebrate the success of Koreans on an international level, and to feel proud of one's Korean North American identity. It is important to maintain a critical and balanced stance toward K-Pop and its success because popular music, such as K-Pop, may carry in its contents elements that are not consistent with the teachings of Christian faith.

Text

Romans 9:1-5

1 *I speak the truth in Christ—I am not lying, my conscience confirms it*

through the Holy Spirit— 2 I have great sorrow and unceasing anguish in
my heart. 3 For I could wish that I myself were cursed and cut off from
Christ for the sake of my people, those of my own race, 4 the people of
Israel. Theirs is the adoption to sonship; theirs the divine glory, the cov-
enants, the receiving of the law, the temple worship and the promises. 5
Theirs are the patriarchs, and from them is traced the human ancestry of
the Messiah, who is God over all, forever praised! Amen.

Questions

1. What does Paul say that he wishes to do for his people (v. 3)? Why does he say that?

2. In light of the passage, is it wrong to have a special affection for one's ethnicity and cultural tradition? Does that special affection conflict with the kind of love that Christians should have for people of all different ethnicities?

Application

What do you personally think of Gangnam Style? What are positive and negative aspects of K-pop from a Korean North American Christian perspective?

27 LESSON

"Sowing and Reaping"

Story

Danny hung up the phone and put his hands on his head. He had no idea what to do. He had been studying for his Spanish test when a couple of guys from class called to tell him that they had stolen the answer sheet off the teacher's desk.

"I can't believe Mrs. Powell left the answer sheet there!" Brad said. "We're all going to my house in an hour to memorize the answers. So, do you want in or what?"

Danny sat at the edge of his bed thinking. He needed to get an A in Spanish in order to keep his GPA above a 3.6. His mom was already hounding him about how he needed to raise it in order to go to college. This would be the easiest way to ensure it. Still, Danny knew cheating was wrong. After five agonizing minutes he decided not to go to Brad's house.

"*I'll just study harder tonight*," he thought to himself.

Questions

1. Do you think Danny made the right choice? Explain.

2. What positive character traits has Danny displayed with his final choice?

Summary

Character is not something we "do" or something we can "use." It is an internal attribute we gain through many decisions we make and many actions we take. In other words, character is a *fruit* of something we have done. Therefore, *every* choice we make is a seed that will bear fruit—our character. Some decisions are big, some are small; some grow in days, others take years. And *when* it grows, not *if* it grows, character will reveal what kind of people we are. For Christians, good character is important because it reveals our identity as God's people.

Text

Galatians 6:7-10

7 Do not be deceived: God cannot be mocked. A man reaps what he sows.
8 Whoever sows to please their flesh, from the flesh will reap destruction;
whoever sows to please the Spirit, from the Spirit will reap eternal life. 9
Let us not become weary in doing good, for at the proper time we will reap
a harvest if we do not give up. 10 Therefore, as we have opportunity, let
us do good to all people, especially to those who belong to the family of
believers.

Questions

1. Seeds can mean and represent multiple things throughout Scripture. What does a seed in Galatians 6 represent? (Hint is in vv. 9-10)

2. In verse 8, Apostle Paul contrasts "sowing to please flesh" with "sowing to please the Spirit." What does he mean?

Food for Thought

Did you know that students who cheat in school are more likely to continue cheating as adults? Statistically, students who cheat in school are 2 times more likely to lie to their boss, and 1.5 times more likely to lie to a significant other.[5]

Application

"Watch your thoughts; they become words.
Watch your words; they become actions.
Watch your actions; they become habits.
Watch your habits; they become character.
Watch your character; it becomes your destiny."

~ André Maurois (*1885-1967*), *French writer*;
(rephrased by Unknown Source)

Share your thoughts on the above quote, and name one desirable and one undesirable action that you keep repeating in your family and school life that could contribute to your character. What can you do in order to encourage the desirable actions and discourage the undesirable actions?

5 Josephson Institute of Ethics. *Study on High School Character and Adult Conduct.* October 29, 2009

28

LESSON

"Keep Out!"

Story

It's been two months since Jason started to attend this church after he moved into the area with his family. Although it was very difficult for him to leave his friends and move to the East coast with his family, hearing from his dad that there is a Korean church near his new home gave him a glimmer of hope that things might not be totally bad after all. From people, to shops, and even climate changes, a lot of things were very different. He felt like a new immigrant in a different country. But he was hopeful that things would be fine when he made new friends in his new home church.

His new church was large, just like the one he attended back on the West coast. But his experience of the youth group in this new church has been very different. Unlike his old church where everyone mingled together like one big family, the youth group in this church seemed like there were different "youth groups" within one large youth group. There were groups that spoke Korean while other groups spoke only English. When Jason tried to take part in their conversations, he got the impression that he wasn't welcome. The students in these groups always sat together, did things together, and seemed very close to each other to the point where it felt like there was no room for him in any group. The youth group as a whole felt very divided, even though they worshipped together every week. Even after two months, Jason still felt invisible and lonely as no one seemed to have taken notice of him and welcomed him into their midst. The hope that Jason had for this church to be his new home away from home ended up as a big disappointment. After two months, Jason decided to try another church where a new friend he met at school was attending.

Questions

1. Can you relate with Jason's difficulty with finding his place in the new youth group? Why do you think it was difficult for him?

2. If you were a member in Jason's new church, what would you have done to help him feel welcomed?

Summary

God created all of us as social beings. This means that the need to belong to a community and the desire to have close friends are natural and important aspect of what it means to be human. By having a sense of belonging and making friends, we find meaning and experience happiness in life. However, even the things that God created to be good for us can turn into something that cause pain and diminish our life. One such example is the friendships we

> **Psalm 133:1**
>
> How good and pleasant it is when God's people live together in unity!

share becoming a clique where, instead of saying "yes" to others, we begin to say "no;" thereby becoming exclusive and self-centered. The negative consequences of forming cliques can be many. One of them is that we become a poor witness of Jesus Christ to others.

Text

Ephesians 2:14-18

[14] For he himself is our peace, who has made the two groups one and has
destroyed the barrier, the dividing wall of hostility, [15] by setting aside in his
flesh the law with its commands and regulations. His purpose was to cre-
ate in himself one new humanity out of the two, thus making peace, [16] and
in one body to reconcile both of them to God through the cross, by which
he put to death their hostility. [17] He came and preached peace to you who
were far away and peace to those who were near. [18] For through him we
both have access to the Father by one Spirit.

John 13:34-35

[34] "A new command I give you: Love one another. As I have loved you, so
you must love one another.
[35] By this everyone will know that you are my disciples, if you love one
another."

Questions

1. According to Ephesians 2:14 and 16, what did Jesus accomplish by dying on the cross? How is what Jesus did the opposite of what people do when they create cliques?

2. According to John 13:34-35, creating cliques can have a huge spiritual implication in our life as Christians, especially in our effort to bear true witness of Christ to others. Why? Can you explain?

Application

1. *Break into groups of three or four, and discuss the following and share together:*
What are the characteristics of cliques? How do you know when something is a clique or just a circle of close friends? What can we do to prevent or discourage cliques from being formed?

2. In public buildings and places, we often come across signs that say, "Drug Free Zone," "Bully Free School," or "Smoke Free Building." Would you dare to claim your youth group as "Clique Free Youth Group?"

Divide into a group of three or four and do the following:
Draft together a Youth Group Pledge to make your youth group a "Clique Free Youth Group." Create a logo and make a poster. Be sure to be creative. Report back and share your work with other groups.

29

LESSON

"What is Prayer Anyway?"

Story

Rose slouched down in the pew for the Easter Sunday worship service with her parents. She sighed and closed her eyes as one of the elders walked up to the podium to pray. As he read out his long and eloquent prayer, Rose could not keep her mind from wandering. All of the prayers recited at church seemed so repetitive and structured. She wondered, "*Am I supposed to pray like that, too? Would God still hear my prayers if I wasn't as articulate with my words?*" Rose continued to reflect as the elder's prayer dragged on. She remembered feeling uncomfortable listening to all of the adults shouting their prayers in unison. They called it a "tong-sung" prayer, but Rose thought it should be called "angry" prayer instead. And what is the deal with praying at 5 o'clock in the morning? There were a lot of things about prayer that Rose didn't understand. She had tried praying before, but it didn't seem to change anything. What was the point of praying if God already knew everyone's needs and futures? She felt a nudge on her shoulder and opened her eyes. As her parents gave her a disapproving look, Rose asked herself one final question, "*What is prayer, anyway?*"

Questions

1. Why do you think Rose felt confused and frustrated with "prayer"?

2. Have you ever asked yourself questions that Rose was asking herself? As a Korean North American, what is your experience with prayers at church or at home?

Summary

When you meet someone you would like to have as your friend, how do you go about developing that friendship? You would try to initiate a conversation. You would ask questions to learn about that person and also talk about yourself. The more you converse with that person, the closer the relationship will be. The closer the relationship becomes, the more you would share. Similarly, prayer simply is having a conversation with God. As conversations develop friendships, prayer brings us to a close relationship with God.

Psalm 13 is a wonderful example of an intimate prayer. Looking at how the psalmist expresses his feelings to God as he is talking to a best friend, we can learn to be genuine and open when we pray. We can learn that being honest in our prayers is surrendering ourselves to God, and that it is through surrender that God transforms us.

Text

Psalm 142

A maskil of David. When he was in the cave. A prayer.

1 I cry aloud to the LORD; I lift up my voice to the LORD for mercy.
2 I pour out before him my complaint; before him I tell my trouble.
3 When my spirit grows faint within me, it is you who watch over my way.
In the path where I walk people have hidden a snare for me.
4 Look and see, there is no one at my right hand; no one is concerned for me.
I have no refuge; no one cares for my life.
5 I cry to you, LORD; I say, "You are my refuge, my portion in the land of the living."
6 Listen to my cry, for I am in desperate need;
rescue me from those who pursue me, for they are too strong for me.
7 Set me free from my prison, that I may praise your name.
Then the righteous will gather about me because of your goodness to me.

Questions

1. What can you say about the tone or manner of this prayer?

2. This prayer is one of the common Biblical prayers. What can we learn about the nature of prayer from this Psalm? How is it similar to and different from the prayers Rose experienced in her church?

Application

What problems, fear, or worries do you need to turn over to God? What praise or thanks do you have to give God? Take a few moments to record your prayer to God.

30

LESSON

"Body Heart Image"

Story

Girl's Story

I have been going through my closet for thirty minutes now. I look so fat and ugly in all these outfits! I shouldn't have eaten those cookies last night. After an hour of scrambling through the clothes and dabbing on some makeup, I rushed downstairs and found mom and her friends talking over coffee. As soon as I saw them, I bowed my head and said, "*Anyong haseyo.*" As usual, the bow was responded to with questions and remarks on my appearance: "*Did you gain some weight? Did you lose some weight? Your hair is getting really long! With all that makeup, you look so grown up.*" Sarah tried her best to maintain her smile and wondered if making comments about weight is a Korean way of greeting somebody.

Boy's Story

I have been eating chicken breast and drinking protein shakes for most of my meals for the last few weeks. I have also been running and lifting weights for two hours every day. I'm doing everything that I can to put on more muscle and lose fat. I hope I can make myself grow taller, too. Well, I don't have control over my height, but I do have the ability to improve my physique. My Caucasian friend Jim gets so much attention from our peers now that he is so muscular. I admit it; I want to look as good as Jim. I want to get those kinds of reactions and compliments, too. I don't want to end up like my dad. Am I doomed to be a small, short, and skinny Korean man like him?

Questions

1. Based on the story, what are the girl's and boy's understandings of beauty and attractiveness? What do you think about their views? Do you agree or disagree?

2. Have you, or someone you know, had a similar experience? Have you ever been discontent/unhappy with your body? Share your experience with the group.

Summary

In our culture, we are continually bombarded with an ideal body image. As we watch a movie, look at the display windows of stores, and go to a gym to exercise, we cannot hide the desire to look a certain way. We feel shameful and depressed after looking at thin, beautiful models on magazine covers or tall, handsome actors on television. We want to look as attractive and beautiful as they are by losing weight, growing taller, or becoming more muscular. We not only judge ourselves but others, too, by their physical appearance. Our society sees overweight people as lazy and agrees short people are outcasts. Influenced by the cultural portrayal of beauty, we have become obsessed with how we look on the outside.

In the story of how David becomes king over Israel, we will notice that God's standards of assessing people differ from ours.

Text

1 Samuel 16:1-13

1 The LORD said to Samuel, "How long will you mourn for Saul, since I have
rejected him as king over Israel? Fill your horn with oil and be on your way;
I am sending you to Jesse of Bethlehem. I have chosen one of his sons to
be king."
2 But Samuel said, "How can I go? If Saul hears about it, he will kill me."
The LORD said, "Take a heifer with you and say, 'I have come to sacrifice
to the LORD.' 3 Invite Jesse to the sacrifice, and I will show you what to do.
You are to anoint for me the one I indicate."
4 Samuel did what the LORD said. When he arrived at Bethlehem, the elders
of the town trembled when they met him. They asked, "Do you come in
peace?"
5 Samuel replied, "Yes, in peace; I have come to sacrifice to the LORD. Con-
secrate yourselves and come to the sacrifice with me." Then he consecrated
Jesse and his sons and invited them to the sacrifice.
6 When they arrived, Samuel saw Eliab and thought, "Surely the LORD's
anointed stands here before the LORD."
7 But the LORD said to Samuel, "Do not consider his appearance or his
height, for I have rejected him. The LORD does not look at the things people
look at. People look at the outward appearance, but the LORD looks at the
heart."
8 Then Jesse called Abinadab and had him pass in front of Samuel. But
Samuel said, "The LORD has not chosen this one either." 9 Jesse then had
Shammah pass by, but Samuel said, "Nor has the LORD chosen this one." 10
Jesse had seven of his sons pass before Samuel, but Samuel said to him,
"The LORD has not chosen these." 11 So he asked Jesse, "Are these all the
sons you have?"
"There is still the youngest," Jesse answered. "He is tending the sheep."
Samuel said, "Send for him; we will not sit down until he arrives."
12 So he sent for him and had him brought in. He was glowing with health
and had a fine appearance and handsome features.
Then the LORD said, "Rise and anoint him; this is the one."
13 So Samuel took the horn of oil and anointed him in the presence of his
brothers, and from that day on the Spirit of the LORD came powerfully upon
David. Samuel then went to Ramah.

Questions

1. In verse 6, when Samuel saw Eliab, he assumed that he would be the next king. Why do you think Samuel made this assumption?

2. Read verse 7. Why did God ultimately choose David to be king?

Application

From what you learned in this lesson, what do you think is God's view of beauty? How does this change your existing view of beauty?

31

LESSON

"Get Even"

Story

Kristen was mortified and could not bear to make eye contact with anyone. Last week she had told Emily a secret: that she had a crush on Bobby, a guy in their Algebra class. Then during lunch today, Kristen was waiting in line for her meal when she overheard Emily telling a group of girls about Kristen's crush. Even worse, Emily told the girls that Kristen had "no chance" with Bobby. Kristen's face turned red and her eyes filled with tears. "*How could I be so stupid to trust her?*" she thought. She was angry at Emily, but acted as though she hadn't overheard anything. Instead, she quickly paid for her meal and sat down at a table by herself. As she slowly ate her pizza, Kristen took sweet pleasure in thinking up ways to get back at Emily. After all, she knew that Emily had a crush on Ricky. An eye for an eye, right?

Questions

1. What did Emily do that upset Kristen?

2. How would you feel if you were in Kristen's shoes? What would you do if you were in Kristen's situation?

Summary

In this story, Kristen is betrayed by her close friend, Emily. Kristen is angry with Emily and starts plotting revenge to hurt Emily in the same way she had been hurt. It is important to emphasize that Kristen is not "wrong" for feeling angry or hurt. What would be detrimental for Kristen, however, is if she were to hurt Emily on purpose out of her own hurt. As Christians, we can demonstrate wisdom in how we handle conflicts and seek reconciliation of broken relationships.

Text

Ephesians 4:26-27

26 "In your anger do not sin": Do not let the sun go down while you are still angry, 27 and do not give the devil a foothold.

Questions

1. Does this verse imply that anger itself is sinful?

2. What does this verse seem to say about holding a grudge?

Application

With your group, come up with three practical tips that would help Kristin deal with her anger, and not become vengeful.

1.

2.

3.

32

LESSON

"Does God Only Love Koreans?"

Story

Lisa took her lunch tray and without hesitation headed over to the table where she ate lunch with the same group of friends since middle school. They were high school boys and girls who were all very much like her: 1.5 and second generation, church-going Korean Americans with nearly perfect GPAs. Lisa felt very comfortable sitting with this group of friends because they understood each other. Besides, when she looked around the cafeteria, other students were all sitting by their ethnic groups: The Latino table, the African-American table, the White table, and the Middle-Eastern table. However, Lisa's world organized by color started to crumble when she met Sasha at the homeless shelter where her church volunteered every once awhile. Although she is a shy Latina, Lisa somehow hit it off with her. Maybe it was because they were the same age. Or maybe because they were big fans of ice hockey, or maybe because Lisa found out Sasha had lost her brother to a car accident just the way Lisa lost her sister when she was young. Sasha shared with Lisa how God helped her through the difficult time. Lisa was truly touched by Sasha's faith although she was Catholic. Lisa never knew that she would have so much in common with a homeless teenager with a totally different cultural background. At the same time, Lisa learned from Sasha that there is much to learn and enjoy from the Latino culture such as music, history, food and a strong sense of community and hospitality. The next day at lunch, despite the curious stares from her Korean friends, she courageously carried her tray to an African American table and pulled a chair next to Melva, who sat next to her in Geometry class, and struck up a conversation with her.

Questions

1. What did Lisa learn after talking with Sasha and getting to know her?

2. If you were Lisa's friend sitting at the Korean table, how would you have viewed Lisa's decision to sit with Melva at the African American table?

Summary

Korean churches in North America have played an important role in cultivating Christian faith for many Korean North American youths. However, these churches sometimes may have led youth unintentionally to become exclusive and reluctant to interact with people of different ethnic and racial background. But our understanding of God who celebrates diversity calls us to make conscious effort to open ourselves to people of different culture and even religion.

Text

Acts 10:9-22

9 About noon the following day as they were on their journey and ap-
proaching the city, Peter went up on the roof to pray. 10 He became hungry
and wanted something to eat, and while the meal was being prepared,
he fell into a trance. 11 He saw heaven opened and something like a large
sheet being let down to earth by its four corners. 12 It contained all kinds of
four-footed animals, as well as reptiles and birds. 13 Then a voice told him,
"Get up, Peter. Kill and eat."
14 "Surely not, Lord!" Peter replied. "I have never eaten anything impure or
unclean."
15 The voice spoke to him a second time, "Do not call anything impure that
God has made clean."
16 This happened three times, and immediately the sheet was taken back
to heaven.
17 While Peter was wondering about the meaning of the vision, the men
sent by Cornelius found out where Simon's house was and stopped at the
gate. 18 They called out, asking if Simon who was known as Peter was
staying there.
19 While Peter was still thinking about the vision, the Spirit said to him,
"Simon, three men are looking for you. 20 So get up and go downstairs. Do
not hesitate to go with them, for I have sent them."
21 Peter went down and said to the men, "I'm the one you're looking for.
Why have you come?"
22 The men replied, "We have come from Cornelius the centurion. He is a
righteous and God-fearing man, who is respected by all the Jewish people.
A holy angel told him to ask you to come to his house so that he could
hear what you have to say."

Questions

1. Why do you think God wanted Peter to go to Cornelius? What does this say about who God is and wants from Christians when it comes to people who are different from us?

2. What prevents people from getting to know people of different racial, cultural and ethnic background? What can we learn from Peter's story?

Application

Rev. Martin Luther King, Jr. once said, "Sunday morning is the most segregated hour of Christian America." Do you think your youth group intentionally embraces differences and diversity? What can you do as a youth group to get to know people of different race, ethnicity, and culture?

Biographies of Editors

Hak Joon Lee is a Professor of Theology and Ethics at Fuller Theological Seminary. He received his Ph.D. (1997, *summa cum laude*) degree from Princeton Theological Seminary and has published several books including: *Covenant and Communication: A Christian Moral Conversation with Jürgen Habermas* (University Press of America, 2006); *We Will Get to the Promised Land: Martin Luther King, Jr.'s Communal-Political Spirituality* (Pilgrim Press, 2006); *Great World House: Martin Luther King and Global Ethics* (Pilgrim Press, 2011); *Bridge Builders* (Doorae Media, 2007); *A Paradigm Shift in Korean Churches* (Holy WavePlus Press, 2011); and numerous articles. He has been a keynote speaker for several celebrations of the Martin Luther King, Jr. Birthday in multiple cities. An ordained Minister of Word and Sacrament in the PC (USA), he founded G2G Christian Education Center, a research institute on Asian-American Christianity and Culture in 2007. With two other Korean American scholars, he published the first systematic curriculum for Korean-American youth, *iDentity: A Curriculum for Korean American Christian Youth*. In 2011, he delivered the Schaff Lectures at Pittsburgh Theological Seminary under the title of "God and Globalization," and served as a fellow at the Christian Leadership Initiative of American Jewish Committee in Jerusalem, Israel.

Kevin Park immigrated to Toronto, Canada from Seoul, Korea just before turning ten years old. He has a B.A. from University of Toronto, M.Div. from Knox College, Th.M. and Ph.D. from Princeton Theological Seminary. He served in various church youth, college, and young adult groups in Canada and the U.S. He was an Adjunct Professor of Theology at New Brunswick Theological Seminary in New Jersey, as well as the Assistant Director of the Asian American Program at Princeton Theological Seminary. For five years, he was the pastor of Bethany Presbyterian Church, a multicultural community in Bloomfield, New Jersey. He also served as an Associate for Theology at the Office of Theology and Worship at the Presbyterian Center in Louisville, KY. He is presently the Associate Dean for Advanced Professional Studies and Assistant Professor of Theology at Columbia Theological Seminary in Decatur, Georgia. He is also one of the authors for *iDentity* (2012). Kevin enjoys his time with his family, who still lives in Louisville—he is looking forward to be reunited with his family in June of 2014. He is married to Irene Yang and they have three daughters, Jubilee, Emily, and Natalie.

Kil Jae Park is a 1.5 generation Korean-American who is bi-cultural and bi-lingual. As an ordained Elder in the United Methodist Church, he is currently the pastor of Teaneck United Methodist Church in Teaneck, NJ—a multiracial, multiethnic, and multicultural congregation. Before taking a full-time appointment in local parish ministry in 2005, he had been a pastor for children, youth and young adult for 18 years. He is a frequent speaker at retreats for Korean American youth and college students and leads numerous workshops and seminars for parents and teachers in many Korean American churches on the topics related to Korean American identity formation and Christian Education. He is also one of the authors for *iDentity* (2012). He is an avid golfer who is happily married to Jee Young, and they are parents of two boys, Jeremy and Daniel.